James P. Covington
5/24/81

D1446400

MAKING IT TOGETHER

MAKING IT TOGETHER

A Survival Manual
for the Executive Family

Ronya and George Kozmetsky

THE FREE PRESS
A Division of Macmillan Publishing Co., Inc.
NEW YORK

Collier Macmillan Publishers
LONDON

Copyright © 1981 by The Free Press
 A Division of Macmillan Publishing Co., Inc.

All rights reserved. No part of this book may be reproduced or transmitted in any form or by any means, electronic or mechanical, including photocopying, recording, or by any information storage and retrieval system, without permission in writing from the Publisher.

The Free Press
A Division of Macmillan Publishing Co., Inc.
866 Third Avenue, New York, N.Y. 10022

Collier Macmillan Canada, Ltd.

Library of Congress Catalog Card Number: 80-69284

Printed in the United States of America

printing number

1 2 3 4 5 6 7 8 9 10

Library of Congress Cataloging in Publication Data

Kozmetsky, Ronya.
  Making it together.

  1. Executives—United States—Family relationships.
2. Married people—Employment—United States.
3. Life skills—United States. I. Kozmetsky,
George, joint author. II. Title.
HF5500.3.U54K69 1981   646.7'8   80-69284
ISBN 0-02-917910-6

To Greg, Nadya, and George

Contents

Preface

For some years we have taught a non-credit graduate-level seminar at The University of Texas at Austin on the subject of executive futures. To accelerate understanding of the topics to be raised in class discussion, we have used a teaching syllabus, complemented by current readings.

The rationale for the seminar, and for this book, the outgrowth of our syllabus, is that nothing in the normal graduate business school curriculum prepares prospective business leaders for the realities of life approaching the top. And, far from being a problem to be faced in some dimly perceived future, the pressures of top management are imminent—in fact, many of today's young men and women will be experiencing life well up on the corporate ladder within two to five years after leaving school. Some of our students have become corporate vice-presidents within five years of graduation!

Recognizing both the reality and the immediacy of the problem, several other universities and a significant number of corporations have joined us in offering this type of course for young executive couples. Their training programs, like ours, are intended as an aid to understanding the required balance necessary to

achieve both family and business goals with a minimum of alienation, anxiety, and disruption.

We deeply appreciate the time, patience, and dedication of
Joanne St. John, who did an excellent job of editing this book. A
special thank you to all our former executive futures seminar students. Without their participation this book would not have been
possible.

MAKING IT
TOGETHER

Introduction:
Why This Book?

In an executive family, where the pressures are greater than average, the chances for unhappiness are also greater. But failed marriages, mid-life career burnout, and corporate wives hooked on Valium are pathetic and needless casualties of life. Any executive couple with courage and commitment to each other—and the willingness to work as hard at marriage as they would at a career—can be successful, and the rewards are immeasurable.

This book is a survival manual for executive families. Many problems associated with success in a management and leadership career are hard to imagine until they occur. For a young couple struggling through graduate school or the beginning work stages of a career, it is difficult to visualize a day when affluence will become a source of tension and family strife; when the executive's career decisions will have to take precedence over cherished family plans; when a move to an exotic country might pose a threat to marital stability; when the executive's success may threaten to destroy a spouse's self-image and confidence; when the executive's overwhelming work schedule will isolate the family from treasured friends and relatives and even from one another; when prolonged separations will be essential to fulfillment of obligations, but inexplicable to small children and concerned friends and neighbors; or when the social pressures of moving among the famous might threaten the emotional stability of a beloved and supportive spouse. Yet, please believe us, these are typical of the problems that most, if not all, top-level executive families must face and must cope with *together* if they are to survive at all. The ability of the family to survive and to grow strong in the face of these pressures may rest in qualities commonly ascribed to the successful executive: innate ability, quick and accurate perceptions, tenacity and commitment, and the almost infinite capacity for adjustment.

At the end of each chapter, we have written a scenario of events some of you might experience in your careers. We call this Executive Future Challenges. In each case, the example is based on a real situation we have known. When in the future, you experience one or several parallel courses of events, you may draw on these Executive Future Challenges to help you solve your real-life dilemmas. Your own solution will be a reflection of the special creativity you bring to your career and to your executive family.

Please note, we have made no attempt to provide answers. There are no pat answers. But, equipped with the tools in the chapters that follow, the two of you together can arrive at your own "right" answers.

We ask executive couples and students reading this book, please trust us once: if you are a prospect for an executive family, take our word that you'll encounter at least some of these problems, and you'll be better off *then* because you're preparing yourselves *now!*

2

Understanding the Leadership Family

Because it is our area of special interest and experience, our frame of reference in this book will be the world of business and management. We are best acquainted with the problems of executives and their families trying to maintain perspective in the face of overwhelming challenges and pressures. Most superperformers in other areas face very similar life experiences. Whatever the leader's specialization, the achievement level involved is extraordinary, and so are the demands—on both the leader *and* their leadership family members.

We don't think the challenges and sacrifices that accompany leadership should come as a surprise to you if one or more members of your family seeks a leadership role. We firmly believe that if you are prepared and are aware of the hazards that lie ahead, you will be better able to cope with the problems when they occur. By anticipating the special demands of leadership, you can improve your family's ability to survive, and you can also discover avenues for making your way of life especially rewarding for every family member. Your enthusiasm for life can become infectious, and can dramatically affect the institutions with which you interact.

The Executive Family: Who Are They, and Why Bother?

When you choose a career in management, and also choose to marry and perhaps have children, the unit that results is unlikely to fit a typical American family model. You will become one of a special tribe—the "executive family." We've observed a great many such families over the years, and have seen why some work for the people involved and why others are disasters. If either of you strives for a top-level executive position, you both might benefit from a preview of some of the events—and attitudes—that will make your own executive family life special.

First, let's meet the members of what we call an executive family. It's usually comprised of one management executive or business entrepreneur, still more typically the male. (More later about nontypical executive families.) Actually he needs very little introduction. The qualities he displays in leading his own corporation ensure him prominence in the community, the state, and the nation. His accomplishments confer on him both status and responsibilities. He is in a position to influence the society he lives in through his actions and through the attitudes he conveys. Then there is his wife, and usually their children, whose lives are influenced in a very real and permanent way by the demands and rewards associated with unusually high achievement. In most executive families (those on which we focus in this book), from the day the budding young executive first goes off to business, a new family relationship exists.

In a conventional executive marriage, where the husband and father is the chief breadwinner and the corporate aspirant, family and social pressures are focused on the woman who has suddenly become an "executive wife." While her husband is involving himself in the executive process, for which he has spent years training and to which he brings both dedication and an abundance of specialized knowledge, the wife is left to perform an ill-defined role for which she may have no precedent. Suddenly she may find herself responsible for the daily fulfillment of both adult roles essential to running the home, rearing the children, and relating to the new community. Wives who are included by their husbands in joint decision making concerning their own participation—whether entertaining business associates in their homes or making a career move to some other part of the country or world—are not inclined to feel victims of their husbands' careers. When both members of a couple are committed to career goals, both can appreciate the role of the executive wife as a very special person and a true professional.

As a prospective executive family, the best time for you to adjust to the pressures of business leadership is long before they occur. From the time your special goals and directions are established, you should begin to develop the attitudes that will make those goals attainable within the framework of a healthy relationship. One such attitude concerns the identity of the executive spouse. Both of you had better recognize and respect that identity if it is to be strong enough to withstand the buffeting ahead. Because we can assure you, when one marriage partner is motivated to achieve at a leadership level, both partners (and their children) are subjected to the strains of reaching and existing at that level.

In today's business world the executive spouse can be either male or female, but since men still comprise the majority of executives, we will concentrate on the executive wife. She is not a second-class citizen, enslaved to her husband's career or subservient to corporate needs. She may maintain a career of her own outside the home, or she may fulfill her ambitions through artistic expression or by active participation in community affairs. In the finest sense she is *somebody* in her own right. She is also an essential factor in her husband's success, through her understanding and endorsement of his career goals and through her capacity to deal constructively with the special burdens and frustrations that he— and she—must face in achieving them and, occasionally, in failing to do so.

Whether the family members share in the executive's limelight or are lucky enough to have their privacy protected, they are subjected to unusual pressures. The strains upon the family can become intolerable, particularly if the marriage partners fail to anticipate them. These pressures, and the lack of preparation to deal with them, have made executive marriages particularly high-risk relationships.

Earlier we mentioned nontypical executive families. One example is a family in which both partners strive for outstanding achievement in their respective careers. In such cases, the pressures of executive marriages are greatly magnified. We've seen some highly successful arrangements that have been devised by strong and innovative couples who can make a workable private life around careers that keep them thousands of miles apart. In one such family the woman executive was appointed to a high Washington post. She lived in the capital and commuted thousands of miles almost every weekend to be at home with her husband (a top manager in a corporation) and their four children. Their arrangement was neither typical nor possible for most married couples, but for them and their family it was a unique way to satisfy both career goals and strong family ties. They managed through extraordinary effort and *giving* to each other to keep their marriage together and to remain a stable, supportive family.

We think that executive families and their special problems are worthy of attention because the people involved in them are significant—not just to one another, but to the corporate families whose lives they influence, to the community, and in the future to the nation and the world. Increasingly successful business executives are dynamic people deeply involved in the larger society, as well as in their own specialized areas. The most successful of them are extraordinarily creative: to become a top-level executive in a major corporation requires an abundance of talent and ingenuity. Management creativity—the ability to perceive a problem differently and to combine elements of a commonly recognized problem in creating an innovative solution—is of the same order as the creativity of great scientists, musicians, and painters. What is considered genius in an artist is frequently dismissed as shrewdness in an executive, but the same creative insights are involved.

In a corporate environment there is often a thin line between success and failure. Frequently, success is the direct reflection of the top executive's gift for making more correct decisions in a business situation. Creative business executives routinely do the impossible, and quietly change history. They are often unknown outside their industries—but the rest of us probably live more comfortable lives because of their achievements. We think that the lives of the families that support and reinforce these special people are well worth consideration and understanding.

A major difference between creative executive leaders in business, government, and academia and their counterparts in the arts is that executives are held accountable for their decisions and actions, and often for those of their subordinates. Not only moral and economic sanctions but legal sanctions as well may be invoked against an executive who goes astray in the interpretation or execution of his responsibilities. In recent years the communications media have painted a vivid picture of the fate of top-level leaders who make wrong decisions—even for what they consider right reasons. Though such accountability is a fact of life for business leaders, it is still a source of pressure to which other creative professionals and critics are not subjected.

One of the hazards in business today is that the rules change without warning. Business leaders who think they have behaved in a responsible fashion can find themselves accused of improper behavior. An illustration of this risk can be seen in the current tax laws, such as the Tax Reform Act of 1976. Corporations are forced to reorganize completely their past attitudes and practices relating to expense accounts and gift giving. Lavish expenditures that were legal and ethical last year are not only illegal, but immoral this year! In the confusion occasioned by the rush to reform, many small industrial concerns have been forced to hire in-house tax attorneys just to stay legal. Business leaders wouldn't dare to trust their own interpretations of these changing rules, even if they could keep up with the changes.

It becomes especially important for leaders, subjected as they are to the tensions and loneliness of incredibly demanding professional lives, to enjoy a stable, harmonious, and generally supportive home environment in which they are able to relax and in which they are not judged as they are by the outside world. The marriage partner who can protect the executive—and the family—against outside intrusions, and who can offer reinforcement and acceptance in the face of chaos, can do much to counter the negative impact of public life. Sadly, too few leadership families acknowledge the need for such internal protection soon enough to avoid being scarred.

Time Is the Essence

Time compression has become a significant fact in your life, whether or not you recognize it. We speak of "how fast children grow up these days," or remark that "it seems like yesterday that gas was 27¢ a gallon!" In these comments we acknowledge an undescribed influence on our lives: the world is changing faster in contemporary times than it ever has before. We might make a convincing case for a new generational cycle of five years, instead of the conventional two decades. Because of the effects of time compression, we can no longer think of a generation in traditional terms. Since 1963 we've been through the Beatles generation, the protest generation, the nostalgia generation, and we are now witnessing the coming of age of a vocationally oriented generation. Would you be willing to predict what the next five years will bring? Just contrast today's college students with those whose protests filled the media a few years ago! Don't you see a generation gap? Ten years ago ROTC centers and military recruitment booths were bombed and picketed. Today many students and other young people actively seek permanent careers in the military.

As a result of time compression, you can gain in just a few years the experience that might have taken your grandfather a lifetime to amass. If you are unable to assimilate that experience and move on to a new plateau, you could become a casualty of modern society. Alvin Toffler has described this as *Future Shock,* the title of his compelling and often frightening book. One of the most disturbing points Toffler makes is summed up in a quote from Dr. Robert Hilliard of the Federal Communications Commission: "At the rate at which knowledge is growing, by the time the child born today graduates from college, the amount of knowledge in the world will be four times as great. By the time that same child is fifty years old, it will be 32 times as great, and 97 percent of everything known in the world will have been learned since the time he was born." * If the implications of this statement are staggering for those of us who enjoy life in the quiet of the mainstream, think

* From *Future Shock* by Alvin Toffler, Random House, New York, N.Y., 1970.

what it means for leaders who must guide us through the turbulent future!

Nowhere will time compression be more real than in your life as an executive. Going into a management career today, you must be prepared to have your goals, opportunities, and decisions colored by rapid changes in the external world. You may achieve in just a few years out of school what once might have been a lifetime goal. A current adage in one graduate school of business is that school prepares the graduate for the first one or two jobs: from then on, it's up to the individual's own professionalism in management. In everyday terms, that means if you're an executive with ambitions to rise to the top, you must have the capacity to apply your formal schooling, on-the-job training, intuition, growing management skills, plus whatever innate talent you possess, and on top of that you must be extremely adaptable in order to solve problems that aren't company-specific or even industry-specific, and that may not even have been defined in the good old days when you were still in graduate school!

As recently as twenty years ago a business graduate could reasonably expect to enter an industry, learn its special characteristics, display leadership talents, and then spend a working lifetime as a specialist-manager in that industry. But in those two decades, our technological society has exploded tradition. Whole industries have disappeared, and other giants have taken their place. These changes have occurred in response to new scientific understandings, technological achievements, and changes in social and cultural attitudes and expectations—a formidable combination indeed!

Consider the fate of the railroads in the United States. With the advent of fast, inexpensive air travel and cheap gasoline for private automobiles and trucks, the great American railroad system faded from glory and in fact came within a hairsbreadth of complete obsolescence. Yet at the very time the railroads were curtailing their schedules and allowing rolling stock to deplete through attrition, the world was tumbling over the brink of the energy crisis. Gasoline and diesel fuels have become so scarce and so prohibitively expensive that the mighty trucking industry is threatened. Personal travel by automobile is now a luxury. Yet our demand for delivery of goods and services has remained undiminished, and the railroads appear today to offer an economical means to keep America moving!

As a contemporary executive, you may actually rise to the top in two or three widely different careers over a thirty-year working lifetime. Increasingly, you new leaders will be functional specialists—experts not in a particular industry or technology, but rather in solving a class of management problems that might occur in any business, academic, or governmental organization. Time compression will put additional pressures on you not merely to keep up, but to sharpen your visionary skills and to lead and direct change, or to prevent or retard it.

Taking the Shock out of Executives' Futures

What this means to your executive family is that all of the tensions built up while the executive deals with pressures in professional life must somehow be let off at home. Obviously, if there is no strong family framework to withstand this letting-off of steam, serious problems can result. In addition to the personal stresses that must be channeled, there are actual changes that you all must share: geographic relocation, drastic alteration of income, social status, freedom of movement, and sudden visibility to the outside world. Your own family, without even changing its emotional and social attitudes and perceptions, may be viewed and treated as ambitious and avaricious, as reserved and snobbish, as admirable or (more frequently) enviable, or as ruined and pitiable—all because of changes in the executive's role in the corporation and the community, and your appearance of upward or downward mobility.

It has been our experience that many families who must share these changes with an upcoming young executive do *not* share the executive's anticipation and understanding of them. The suddenness of these changes, plus the new attitudes outsiders may express toward them, have thrown many an executive family into a bad case of "present shock." While the changes and attitudes themselves are often unavoidable, the element of surprise *is*.

No family should have to face unprepared the trauma that struck close friends of ours. In a very short time our friends moved from a modest lifestyle to one of considerable affluence. For some years, the husband had practiced his original profession, and the family lived comfortably on the income from that career. When he decided to change careers, entering a business involving the development of new communities, he became both very successful and extremely affluent. While the family's social values and ethics didn't change, their economic situation did. Many of their long-time acquaintances were unable to accept this fact.

From their friends' perspective, the family simply didn't behave as successful business families should. Because of this family's new economic status, even fairly intimate friends reacted with either formality or embarrassment. The family members were bewildered, then very disturbed, because they couldn't cope with the roles that were being imposed upon them. When, some years later, the new business suffered economic reverses and went into bankruptcy, the family experienced another shock. Now they were expected to assume a new role, suitable to their fallen situation. Through all of the changes—the sudden success, the eventual economic reversal—the family remained basically the same, but others were quite unable to see them in this light. They were victims not of their actual experience, so much as of their failure to conform to the roles their friends expected and demanded that they play.

We contend that the kinds of ups and downs our friends experienced are not unusual—for executive families—nor should they necessarily be traumatic. While outside pressures can often have a devastating effect, *as a prepared family* you can counter negative influences fairly effectively. What is important is that you are in harmony with one another, that you understand and respect one another's goals—even when you do not share them—and that you learn to cope with change. The ability to turn negatives into positives is one characteristic you must learn if you are to be a successful executive family.

An important prerequisite of this ability is to recognize at the *beginning* of your business life that your family situation will never be typical, and that it will not conform to the standards established and expected by the outside world. Many of the problems that you will face, once you understand and anticipate them, can either be avoided entirely or can at least be minimized when they occur. Others that can neither be avoided nor minimized can be dealt with more effectively when they *do* occur because they will not come as a surprise. Some graduate schools of business and corporations, recognizing the unusual forces that operate within management families, have joined us in offering seminars for prospective executives like yourselves. These seminars explore some of the special problems and introduce tools that have been used effectively by older executive families in coping with such problems.

Many young couples look at their future executive or leadership career in the abstract, without any real sense that what we discuss in seminars can really happen to them. And a lot of them find out fairly quickly that what we're talking about is the *real* world!

One young couple who had recently gone through our executive futures seminar had occasion a few months ago to try out what they had learned. The husband had been a graduate student in management, and he moved very quickly out of school into corporate life, and up the ladder to the vice presidency of a large casualty insurance company. A series of problems besieged the company's management, and eventually the company was forced into bankruptcy. The young vice president found himself with substantial financial commitments, and with a short track record already tainted with a failed company. Initially, he and his wife went into a period of shock and depression. Luckily they both remembered that they had been forewarned to expect such a setback *at least once* in their career. What they needed to do was figure how to turn this particular negative experience into some kind of positive opportunity for their future. One thought emerged: While going through the trauma of the company's financial devastation, the husband had become unusually knowledgeable about the specific pitfalls that might face companies expanding rapidly in the casualty insurance field. He learned of a national conglomerate that had recently entered the field of casualty insurance, and he presented his case to them: he knew what could happen without considerable experience in his uncharted area, and he was uniquely equipped to save them costly errors. He so impressed top management that he was offered an excellent executive position with the conglomerate, and an opportunity to turn his unhappy personal experience to both a personal and a new corporate advantage. Five years later he was president of the conglomerate's insurance company.

Again, while our focus in this book is on problems that occur in a specialized area, the world of business and management, the problems themselves—and the tools for dealing with them—are virtually identical for leaders in most social institutions. Our objective in this book is to suggest a framework within which you, as a leadership couple in any field, can start out as a commonly striving unit, can operate harmoniously over a working lifetime, and can emerge after children are grown and professional responsibilities diminished as a loving and fulfilled pair of individuals still moved by mutual respect and admiration. Society eventually expects *all* leaders to pay dues, and you will too. But you can keep the personal cost down if you work at it consciously.

A chaplain of a renowned girls' school talked to participants in a seminar on the deteriorating American family. His perceptions differed from those of many participants, and he reflected happily on his marital career. His comments suggest how a couple can grow in happiness and fulfillment over many years of marriage, rather than drawing apart over time. He said, "I have been married three times already, and probably I will be married at least four times before I die. However, I must make a note here that I have been married to the same woman each time."

He went on to explain that periodically during their long married life, he and his wife have taken stock, readjusted, and looked at how each has changed. Both partners *have* changed, but by being attuned to one another, and by making periodic evaluations of how the changes in one affect the other, they have been sensitive to alterations that the passage of time and their individual experiences have produced in their relationship. The reexamination and recommitment have allowed them to bring their individual growth into the marriage to enrich it. Each time, they can look forward to further interest and satisfaction from the union, because each time *new people,* revitalized by experience and growth, are entering it. With all the growing each has done separately, and both have done together, they can look forward to sharing old age with the same mutual commitment they brought to their "first marriage."

Looking back from our vantage point of more than thirty-five years of happy, but not untroubled marriage, we have seen the couple's happy experience repeated over and over again by people we have known. In each case, their secret seemed to be a conscious striving to bring excitement and vitality into the marriage on a daily basis. While it doesn't come easy, we believe that you can achieve such a rewarding relationship if you start in your twenties or thirties to work together toward a meaningful and vital marriage, both deliberately recharging your emotional batteries. With such mutual and purposeful effort, you can look forward to arriving at age sixty or sixty-five with the same enthusiasm and zest for life together that you enjoy in your youth. It is important to realize that, like many executives, you can come into the business world as a family, and you can also emerge as a family.

Being always conscious of yourself as a couple, assessing your personal growth and your changing relationship over time, is an effective technique for building a long-lasting and satisfying marriage. In the next chapter we'll discuss related techniques that can help you to stay on target as an executive family.

EXECUTIVE FUTURE CHALLENGES

We have discussed in the preceding chapter several examples of real situations lived through by ourselves or people we know. Believe it or not, you will find yourself at some point in situations comparable to these. Take the time to consider how you, your spouse, and your children might handle the following.

1. You (husband) are an executive who has been very successful in a large and stable corporation. You've now been offered the presidency of a small, struggling company that has an excellent product but, due mainly to poor management, is on the verge of bankruptcy. You and your wife have four small children, and you've looked forward to your secure future in the large corporation, but it would take you years there to advance to the CEO position. The new position would afford you that status immediately *if* you could turn the company around. If you could not achieve such results, you would be out of a job, and in the position of having to start again from the bottom—this time with a record of failure. How would you (wife) approach this problem? As an executive family how would you deal with it?

2. In a period of five years, you have become extremely successful in your corporation. You have been thrust into a position of prominence in the community. Your spouse has not kept up, either socially or intellectually, with your development and rapid rise. How can *you* help your mate gain self-confidence in this new dimension? How can you maintain equilibrium in your household? Is your spouse's adjustment your responsibility?

3

A Systems Approach
to Families

S. A.
Systems analyst

We've taken a concept spawned by the computer generation and applied it to understanding families. Widely used by mathematicians, engineers, sociologists, political scientists, and business theorists, this new approach to how things work is called *systems analysis*. Unfortunately, a simple definition has *not* accompanied the wide application of the concept. However, one fairly satisfactory way to explain systems analysis is that it looks at a process or an experience as an integrated whole and tries to explain why the whole world (or system) works as it does. In this sense, microorganisms, people, computers, organizations, the universe—and the family—can all be viewed as systems and can be studied in a similar fashion. Families are, after all, groups of individuals existing in a special kind of relationship to one another, and considered in a special frame of reference. When two people marry, in our terms they become a family system. Using the systems lexicon, any children born into that family can be considered subsystems of the family system.

What is important about viewing families in systems analysis terms is that the study is not abstract or academic. The whole purpose of systems analysis is to understand *and modify* the work-

17

ing of a system. Thus, the tools of systems analysis provide a useful means for families to study themselves: to understand how they work, and to help direct what happens to them. This is especially important in understanding changes that inevitably happen to any family. Changes can result from purely natural causes (children becoming more independent as they grow older), or from the deliberate response to outside stimuli (moving to a more affluent neighborhood as income level rises).

Conceptual Tools

In looking at your own and other families as systems, two conceptual tools are especially useful. One is the idea of the "natural hierarchy," and the other is the so-called "cybernetic approach." Hierarchies—the order in which things are put together—occur in nature and in man-made systems, including the family system. And they change over time. Hierarchies in the family involve the intimate relationships among individual family members or subsystems and those among the family and the outside world. Hierarchies also come into play in the changing structure of the family's common objectives over time. Intimate family relationships change in response to growth and aging, and also in response to changes in the external world, and so they must be considered at various points in terms of the total life-span of the marriage. The following model suggests, very generally, how both the composition of a family and the relationships within it change over time.

Lifespan	Before 25	25–35	35–45	45–65	After 65
Relationships	Husband/ Wife	Husband/ Wife children ages 1–10	Husband/ Wife children in high school and college	Husband/ Wife	Partner alone

Briefly, what we're saying is that as a childless couple in your early 20s embarking on a first career, you will have a different family structure and very different objectives from those you might have as a twenty-five to thirty-year-old couple with children ranging from toddlers to ten-year olds, and a career moving rapidly toward top management. In either of those periods your family will differ in structure and priorities from what you will be as a thirty-five to forty-five-year-old couple with teenage children, and a position near the top of the executive ladder. And at each of these stages you will differ from what you will become as a couple at your professional peak, or even retired, with children who are grown and away from home. The most dramatic change will occur when one of you dies, and the other is forced to face the challenges of living alone.

Let's consider an actual family over time, namely our own. We were married in our college years, and our honeymoon was interrupted by World War II. Following that, we proceeded to graduate studies at an eastern university, the birth of our first two children, and the commencement of a career in college teaching, all during our mid twenties. In our twenty-five to thirty-five-year-range, we had a third child. One of us, Ronya, worked full time as a homemaker, while the other, George, accepted a second academic post and then left it to launch a new career in industry. During years thirty-five to forty-five, George's industrial career progressed rapidly to top executive ranks, and eventually to the forming of a new company. The children were all in school, and Ronya continued her career as mother, homemaker, and professional wife to a top executive, and in addition, she embarked on a new personal career in teaching.

In these early years our family moved nine times. Our economic status changed from that common to struggling grad students and young college instructors to the affluence enjoyed at the top ranks in an important industry. We progressed from worrying about buying shoes for the babies to struggling to protect our teenagers from the social and emotional pitfalls that beset "rich kids." Between the ages of forty-five and forty-nine, we watched our children start off to college, and then we were free to launch a third set of careers of our *own*. George left industry to explore his longtime interest—a totally new academic pursuit, while Ronya exchanged her teaching profession for a new one in financial management. In our fifties, we can look forward to comfortable retirement, enriched by the many interests we share, and by those each of us has developed independently through the preceding years of growth and change.

While our family may not be typical in the directions of our career choices or in the level of success we've been fortunate enough to attain, it probably is typical in the shifting priorities and interests that each hierarchical time stage produced. At each stage of our career, we consciously applied systems concepts to our family decision making. Although difficult at first, this discipline proved enormously helpful to us as a family.

A systems analysis approach to living is important because it will almost force your family to define its overall objectives. More often than not, families just happen and grow, with no internal communication concerning objectives and directions. In highly motivated upwardly mobile executive families, such as your own, unplanned development could bring about problems and could cause emotional strains. In formulating your goals, it is important to allow for setbacks and disappointments. Remember, wherever there is an objective there is generally also a constraint pulling against achieving that objective. In a systems approach to family living, you must be alert to both objectives and constraints, and whether they remain the same over time, or change as your family progresses and develops from one life stage to another.

In addition to hierarchies, we mentioned a second system analysis tool useful in looking at families: the cybernetics approach. Cybernetics tells us it's all right to ignore what we all learned in school about the process of cause and effect—a logical process not often practical in working with people on a daily basis (especially when some of those people are small children). By applying cybernetics thinking, we don't have to know the cause, or wait for the effect, to decide if a process is effective. *Supposing* becomes a legitimate basis for acting, and permits altering plans and programs in midstream if feedback (observations made along the way) and new data inputs suggest that the desired results aren't being achieved.

In family situations, the systems method means that you may alter any course of action if it doesn't seem to work, with no necessity to pursue it to a logical conclusion. This approach removes many of the inhibitions in formulating and altering family objectives, standards, and strategies: if a goal doesn't seem worth the pain of achieving it, substitute a more realistic goal. Applying this approach and assessing the progress of your family toward established goals, you might realize soon after one of your children enters school that this child doesn't rank among academic super-achievers. Rather than continue your established practice of rewards for As and Bs, you're free to adopt a new system of goals for this child, in which he or she can instead be rewarded for excellence in some other area—sports, music, crafts projects—that allows him or her to achieve the satisfaction of performing successfully.

Such conscious flexibility in setting and moving toward goals will be particularly important to you as an executive family. All members will be free to evaluate the rewards and sacrifices involved in such goals and to measure those against personal attitudes. If situations arise that are counterproductive to the emotional health of your family, you can change them before the pressures become intolerable.

We recently saw this assessment process work for one family. The husband/father was an extremely ambitious young executive who had worked hard to achieve his career goals. In just five years he had become a vice president of his aggressive organization. In order to succeed further, he would have to move his family again —the fourth move to a new part of the country in less than three years. When the company asked him to make the latest move, he and his wife discussed honestly both the significance of another relocation and the impact of a refusal on the husband's future with the company. After much soul searching, they decided together that the emotional stability of their family was more important to them than was his executive ambition. He left his job, and the family moved to a city where he and his wife wanted to put down roots. He has launched a new career as an entrepreneur in a field closely aligned to the one he left, working even harder than before, though earning considerably less. He is unconcerned, however, because he and his wife both feel they have made the right decision for the entire family.

Objectives and the Family System

Systems analysis can teach us some useful lessons on evaluating family objectives and deciding how realistic they are. A typical systems approach is to establish a goal and then work backward from it, trying to list the constraints that will interfere with achieving the objective. Using this technique, you and your family could decide where you want to be in 20 years—in terms of leadership status, economics, and even geography, as well as ethically and emotionally—and then work backward from that ideal, establishing interim objectives that must be met along the way to achieve it, and considering the various constraints that might interfere.

For any particular couple one objective or constraint may assume overwhelming importance over all others. Two friends of ours spent the husband's graduate school years making an exhaustive investigation of the ideal location to make their home and raise their future family. They didn't worry about a particular job, but about finding a job in their chosen city. They wrote to chambers of commerce in all the cities they were considering and made an in-depth survey of those that checked out. Finally by the time the husband had his MBA, they'd made their decision. It was Seattle or no place. Then he inverviewed extensively—and exclusively—in that city until he secured a position. They have lived there for twenty-five years now and have never regretted their somewhat unusual career decision.

If you are like most prospective executive families, the most common constraint in your early years will be money. Another fairly typical constraint is a conflict of careers: if one of you has chosen a field that involved permanent commitment to a particular geographic area, while the other seeks a career that will probably require frequent relocation, this clash of objectives must be discussed and resolved before an actual conflict occurs that could destroy your relationship. In some situations, early recognition and open discussion of incompatible objectives will be enough to resolve misunderstandings; in other cases serious compromises may be necessary on the part of one or both partners.

Today, with our very different perspective on two-career marriages, it is more than ever crucial for you as a couple to deal with potentially conflicting goals and to explore together the prospects for developing each partner's career to the desired level. Systems techniques, applied at the beginning of your relationship, can help to smooth out many potential rough spots. For example, you should reach a decision about which career will be emphasized at a particular point in your family's growth. Bear in mind that such decisions are not unalterable, and in fact should probably be part of the reevaluation you undertake from time to time.

As you start out in marriage, you should devote at least as much time to considering where you want to be in twenty years as you do to your silverware pattern! We know one young two-career couple, both successful professionals, who find themselves approaching their fifth anniversary with diametrically opposed plans for the next few years. They have been living very comfortably on two substantial incomes. Now, as the wife approaches 30, she is actively interested in fulfilling a nesting urge. She is prepared to retire, for a few years at least, and to replace the joys of freedom and a second income with the joys of parenting. Her husband is not only shocked, he's horrified! He is far from achieving his goals for their material comforts, and has no interest in a life filled with more expenses and a lower income. This couple is undergoing a huge strain on their relationship that could have been avoided if they had simply planned together for what they both want from their future.

Two other young friends, former executive futures students, started their careers with a planning session. They agreed to work hard for five years out of school, achieve whatever they could. Then they would start the family they both wanted. The wife would take a leave of absence from her position, spending as many months with their baby as she and her employer agreed were optimum, and then she would return to her career. By the time she became pregnant, she had carefully positioned herself in the organization to ensure her ability to advance, to take an extended absence, and to limit her travel to fit in with her family plans.

After the baby's birth, they felt some pinch from reduced income, but since they had planned for it they had budgeted and didn't find themselves totally strapped. Staying at home with a newborn offered less time for work-related projects than this young mother had anticipated, and while days centered on the baby were unexpectedly pleasant, she found herself spending an increasing number of those days without a sense of any real accomplishment. By the time the baby was four months old, a perfect babysitter was located, the healthy baby was transferred to her care during working hours, and the new mother resumed her career, all according to the couple's predetermined schedule. They feel satisfied that their present five-year plan is workable, and they look forward to expanding their family.

If both of you understand and agree to work toward shared objectives, there is less likelihood of later recriminations because one of you feels victimized by the other's career. Similarly, if you have children who are mature enough to understand family objectives and to be affected by constraints, they should at least have an opportunity to participate in your discussions so that they will not feel repressed by parental dictatorship.

The systems approach to family life can be particularly useful for you as an executive family. To achieve a kind of advance understanding of future problems, and to handle them effectively when they arise, you should consider your business leadership objectives in some detail. How do these objectives relate to the private goals of individual family members? What special constraints might stand in the way of achieving either your common or your individual objectives?

Awareness, conscious attitude and goal adjustment, and constant communication are valuable tools for your leadership family. They are also essential ingredients in a special family relationship discussed in the next two chapters.

EXECUTIVE FUTURE CHALLENGES

In this chapter we have talked about applying systems analysis concepts to your leadership family. We have also mentioned the importance of charting your future together, and some of the parameters that should be plugged in. Position yourself on the chart that follows and try plotting out your future in terms of where you and your family want to be at each age level. Consider the constraints that might interfere: money, career conflicts, relocation.

Age/Level	pre-25	25–35	35–45	45–65	after 65
Career #1 (in or out of home)					
Career #2 (in or out of home)					
Children/no children (if yes, how many)					
Outside involvements church, politics, civic organizations, charities					
Additional education/training					
Geographic location					
Career change (either 1 or 2)					
Income					
Real estate/investments					
Responsibilities to elderly parents, others					
Retirement					
Life alone					

4

Executive Families and the "US" Relationship

We place great emphasis on the creative effort a couple is willing to expend in making a marriage last over the long haul. We've coined a phrase that represents the kind of relationship that can result from such a deliberate mutual effort. We call it an US relationship, and it is well worth the work required to achieve it *if* you are the kind of couple who seriously desire a strong, life-long commitment to one another.

If you're not yet married, and you want an US relationship, an ideal time to begin is now, when you are still exploring together what each of you wants and expects to gain from the marriage. If you can be objective, you may recognize beneath your culturally idealized romantic attachment some other strong reasons for your attraction to one another: your need for companionship, financial and emotional security, sex, children, social acceptability, and even escape. All of these are elements in what can become an US relationship.

If you're already married, chances are you didn't work consciously at establishing common goals before your marriage. So the next best time to begin your US relationship is *right now!*

27

We have seen, over and over, that the pressures of executive life can destroy less solidly based marriages.

And the pressures of executive life are right around the corner. We can't overstate the importance of reaching an understanding at the earliest possible point in your marriage, because the next five years will almost certainly be the most difficult five years in your life as a future executive couple. Without a framework of mutual respect and support, and a shared sense of direction, you could be one of the many couples who fail to survive these years as a functioning family.

Who Is a "Whole ME?"

An US relationship is not for everybody. It is not possible unless the principals are *both* striving to become whole MEs, and both are willing to keep the relationship going. This is not possible without conscious effort. It's not something you achieve and then take for granted. If you are interested in and able to achieve an US, your relationship will change over the years just as you will, but we can guarantee that ten years down the road—or forty—you will still have a meaningful marriage—and friendship.

Now: What is a whole ME? What is an US? In typical schoolyard fashion, ME first! For some reason, the concept of a whole ME is difficult to grasp. Possibly because it's a contextual definition. If I'm a whole ME in my business career, I still may be only a partially realized ME in my family life. If I'm a whole ME when everything is going smoothly, a crisis may cause a reversion to a partially realized ME. And maybe a tragedy will cause a partial ME to become whole. Maturity—and MEness—are not constant states.

Here are some of the qualities former executive futures students have identified as characteristics to strive for if you want to be a whole ME: Have a good self image. Be able to listen—and *hear*—not just talk. Don't seek constant ego gratification. Don't be hung up on instant satisfaction or pleasure. Be trusting (in your marriage and in outside relationships, including your career). Have integrity, compassion, tenderness, empathy, loyalty, discrimination, resiliency, self-security, and a sense of humor. Be giving of self. Be tolerant of and adaptable to change. Be resistant to dogma. Be receptive to other points of view. Have a strong personal ethic.

What a terrific person a whole ME is! No wonder nobody is a whole ME all of the time! But by keeping the goals in mind, each of us can come closer to being a whole ME.

We've said an US requires two whole MEs. Now obviously, if nobody is a whole ME all the time, there's got to be some give and take in this relationship. In the best of all worlds, when one person in a marriage is being a partial ME, the other whole ME will be there to compensate. And at some future date the roles will reverse. But practically, most US relationships are *usually* made up of two sometimes-whole MEs who are striving to do better—for the sake of one another and for their children. Striving to be a whole ME must be a lifetime occupation!

While we can't define an US much more precisely than we defined a whole ME, we can describe in some detail the many ways in which two mature, confident, and giving people can achieve it. First, an US relationship is a *discipline*. It requires work, conscious and sustained effort, from both marriage partners. It requires open and honest discussion—of the kind necessary to exchange information for applying systems techniques, setting and adjusting long-term objectives, considering restraints, assessing progress along the way. An US requires a lifetime of such talking, listening, and really *hearing* one another.

Let's acknowledge right here that there's a vast difference between listening and hearing. Many couples learn this the hard way. When they arrive at a complete breakdown of communication, each accuses the other of not listening. Actually, a great deal of talking *and* hearing is being done by both sides. What nobody is really doing is *listening to* what's being said. "Hearing" is usually done from one's own point of view, filtering content through a set of personal biases. *Real* "listening" means making a conscious effort to understand the *other* person's point of view, forgetting one's own prejudices. The ability to listen to another person is a first step toward full and total communication with that person. This special kind of communication, involving talking and listening, is an essential ingredient of an US relationship.

What Makes an US?

An US relationship can't be precisely defined because it varies from couple to couple and from family to family. The basic rule is to *communicate!* In an US relationship politeness is not a ground rule. The partners are free to interrupt one another—even yell at each other—to express love, anger, fear, embarrassment, pride, or shame without worrying about shocking the other or threatening the relationship. Ideas and prejudices don't have to be concealed. In fact, each partner in an US seeks the comfort of opening up to a supportive listener, and looks to the mate as a security blanket to offer loving protection and reinforcement against the outside world.

The key to achieving such a relationship is: *don't judge one another.* You may disagree with your partner, and object to his or her behavior or attitudes, but why feel compelled to pass judgment or moralize? In an US relationship, either of you can do something stupid or embarrassing and still be confident that *one* person in the world still loves and accepts you—even if you *are* a damned fool! Acceptance of the person doesn't imply approval of the behavior, but it does acknowledge that a person who makes a fool of himself occasionally isn't always a fool, and that one social gaffe isn't a permanent disaster.

In an US relationship, a wife who finds herself out on a limb can let go, because she knows someone will catch her. A husband who makes a stupid decision may be criticized at work, but he knows he can go home and tell his wife "I did a dumb thing, and can't get off the hook." She'll probably agree that what he did was dumb, but she won't stop loving and respecting him. The alternative to such total, loving acceptance is all too apparent.

We've all observed the "Virginia Woolf syndrome"—marriages in which the partners constantly attack and score points off one another's weaknesses. This kind of infighting is destructive to any individual or relationship. It can be particularly devastating in the life of a struggling young executive who is constantly externally threatened and personally pressured to make correct decisions. For such a person the comfort and security of an US relationship at home can mean the difference between success and failure in his or her business life.

Just as the majority of people setting out on a business career have objectives far short of top-level executive positions, so most couples embarking on a marriage can be satisfied with a less demanding—and far less rewarding—kind of relationship. To be able to open up fearlessly to another human being, and to support that person in adversity as well as in success, requires a strong personality, emotional maturity, and self-confidence. That's why an important ingredient of an US relationship is two secure MEs.

An US is not a 50–50 type of association; sometimes one member happily gives 70, 80, or even 90 percent to the other's 30, 20, or 10. The secret is being aware of your partner's need at the moment, and giving what is needed—not necessarily what you want to give. The times when such reciprocal giving is toughest—and when a sense of humor may be your salvation—are those all-too-frequent times when *both* of you need to be on the 80-percent-receiving end. If you can get through those times still laughing together, you're well on the way to an US!

In science there is an analogy to US: the synergistic relationship. Here, the combination of two elements yields a result that is greater than the sum of its parts. In a synergistic—or an US—relationship, one plus one equals more than two. Its value is derived from some unique interaction between the elements that comprise it.

In an executive marriage, the need for a giving relationship becomes apparent very early. In the case of a young executive husband experiencing a job crisis, enormous support and cooperation are required at home. At such times his wife must be able to postpone the gratification of her own needs in order to make their home a haven of peace and tranquility for him. Any wife with small kids underfoot, or with her own career demands outside the home, knows just how much giving it takes to put her husband's needs ahead of her own. But in a real US relationship, she can be secure in the knowledge that *her day will come!* One day, when she needs it most, her husband will be the giving partner, and she can give vent to *her* needs. If the wife has a career outside the home, she, too, will experience job frustrations and will need tender, loving support. A wife who is also the mother of small children will go through periods of cabin fever and frustration that will demand time and understanding from her husband. Perhaps he will do *his* giving by spending a Saturday with the children while his wife takes a day off for herself—and she may even come home to a clean house and clean children! Whatever the special needs, they will be recognized in an US relationship where each partner is attuned to the other, and sensitive to their special relationship.

An US relationship, to work, demands that both partners feel a sense of commitment to the relationship itself. Whatever the sacrifices, setbacks, or separations, *both* must be persuaded that continuing together will be the ultimate and unquestioned outcome. No matter what interruptions occur in their time together, each partner in an US seeks to return to the comfort and security found in the presence of the other. The little model below is our conception of what makes an US relationship: the special contributions of the man and woman over time, reflecting the dynamics of a growing relationship.

$$\frac{\text{HIM} + \text{HER}}{\text{time}} = \text{US}$$

We have watched couples fall into three specific behavior patterns that are especially dangerous to the survival of an US relationship. One is *keeping score*. Trying to achieve a 50–50 balance between giving and taking is totally counterproductive to an US. Contractual marriages often run into difficulty for just this reason. Giving should be in direct relation to need. Both partners must trust that over a lifetime together giving and taking will balance. Totally <u>one-sided giving</u> can also lead to trouble. When one partner always demands, and the other always gives, there is no mutuality of commitment to the relationship, and an US can't really thrive. Sometimes only one partner in a couple is truly working at being a whole ME and the other is still basically insecure and afraid to give freely of self. If *both* can consciously work at achieving mutual trust and giving, an US can possibly develop over the years. Finally, an US relationsip can be seriously threatened if *honest com-*

munication is sacrificed, even in the interest of protecting one another's feelings.

We can attest to the pitfalls of halfway communication from our own early experience. Several years after we were married, our path led us to a graduate school of business in the east. Having less money than ambition, one of us, who shall remain nameless, hit on a scheme for economizing on the cross-country move by buying a trailer to move our worldly goods and then selling the conveyance when we arrived. The other had immediate reservations about the plan, but went along with it rather than cause disappointment. This display of supposed support overcame the schemer's lingering reservations, and we proceeded to act on the plan, each of us managing to convey unfelt enthusiasm and reinforcement for the other.

The trailer was bought, packed, hitched to our car, and off we went. We were *both* secretly apprehensive but putting up a good front. We had driven about a hundred miles when we started climbing into a coastal mountain range. All at once we were dismayed to spot some poor guy's trailer, broken free of its hitch, and running loose at the edge of the road. As we turned to look we were *more* dismayed to recognize the worst: *we* were the poor guy, and it was our trailer crashing over the bank and overturning in a creek bed thirty or forty feet below the road. Through tears, the formerly silent partner was able to point out that the trailer was a lousy idea in the first place, which raised the burning question, "Then why in the hell did you go along with it?" During the lengthy mutual recriminations that followed we both finally saw the light—and swore off white lies as a technique for marital communication. We got our trailer back with only moderate damage to vehicle and contents, and our marriage profited greatly. Ever since this episode, when either of us suspects the other of being less than candid, we ask, "Is this another trailer?" and get one another back on the track!

One strong epoxy glue that can help hold an US together is *humor.* It's impossible to achieve or maintain a smooth-running US if both MEs aren't mature enough to release tension and frustration by laughing at themselves, one another, and life in general. Many times in a marriage the situation appears so grim that nothing seems funny. That's the time when one of you must dig deep to come up with something both can laugh at. Humor lends continuity and form to a relationship. We've watched many marriages fail because the partners have forgotten how to laugh together. Laughter is often the antidote to tears and is certainly a more positive approach to problem solving: if you can go either way, laugh! Our scale in any apparent disaster is always "Are children dying?" If not, the situation can't be too tragic—so relax and laugh!

Children Are Part of US

The sense of the US as a network of mutually supportive and reinforcing individuals should grow if your marriage expands to include children. If you, as parents, are confident of your own worth, you can more readily encourage a child to develop as an individual whose personhood is recognized and appreciated, and who is valued irrespective of sex, birth order, or the traditional social roles assigned girl or boy children. You must work to develop a shared sense of *family* unity, in which children are embraced. Kids must never be outsiders looking in on your US.

As parents you must cultivate a talent for filtering out external influences in order to protect your family's special integrity—what we call "building fences." This aspect of an US relationship is particularly significant to you as an executive family, because you will be different. Since few people in any institution seek leadership status, and fewer still achieve it, the minority of people who do set their goals at a leadership level get little understanding from others. Even well-meaning neighbors, friends, or family members will lack the experience and perspective necessary for real empathy. The special time pressures and strains to which you will be subjected as leaders will be poorly understood, and may evoke from outsiders the kind of criticism that can cause dissatisfaction and pain, especially to children.

If in your situation the husband is the aspiring leader, and the wife the parent who spends more time with the children, it is she who will become the first line of defense for husband and children. Typical of the attacks she must be prepared to face are those solicitious comments directed against the absent husband/father who is "depriving" his family: "What a shame that Joe can't spend more time with you and the kids. At their age they need him so badly," or "Can't you persuade him to stay home more often? After all, work isn't *that* important, and anyway, nobody's indispensable."

We know one wife who got her squelch routine down pat. When some busybody started to sympathize with her plight she'd nip the conversation in the bud by retorting, "Gee, we all think Joe's work *is* important, and right now he's awfully busy. When things ease up, he'll spend more time with us, but for now we figure we're pretty lucky about the *quality* of time he spends with us, so we don't worry about the quantity. When he's here, he's with *us,* not golfing, or playing poker, or watching the tube. And if the kids need somebody in the meantime, *I'm* here, or don't I count?" And this was the message the kids heard, too—not martyrdom, but pride in her husband and their father, and appreciation for the kind of man he was. Both partners in that particular marriage took their parenting seriously. They had built an US relationship and were conscious of making their kids part of it, with a real sense of what the family stood for, and where their goals might lead them.

One useful technique for including children as active partners in an US is to engage them in an ongoing Socratic dialogue. Encourage them to express themselves, to question, and to think as adults. Respond to their questions with still more questions that will help them to think problems through for themselves. Help them learn to formulate and express ideas and discuss those ideas seriously—don't dismiss them because they come from a person who is just a kid.

Children who are not ridiculed or suppressed, whose opinions are considered, and whose mistakes, lapses from logic, and deviations from parental standards don't raise threats of rejection, stand a better than average chance of growing up within the family rather than alienated from it. Especially in leadership families, where external pressures *will* be felt by the children in time, being integrated into a US relationship can provide some measure of protection from the outside world.

Among our circle of close friends is a family that offers a good example of the way in which children can fulfill a meaningful role in an US. This family had a real framework for withstanding unusual pressures and demands. About fifteen years ago the entrepreneur/father became excited about an idea for starting his own company. He was at the time a senior engineer in a large corporation, well situated professionally and financially, and able to offer economic security and comfort to his large family. To quit his job in order to pursue his idea would involve tremendous sacrifices from all of the family. He and his wife had a strong and reinforcing relationship. They examined frankly what the change would mean to the family, and decided together to risk it. When they called the family together they explained to them both the excitement of the future, and the realities of the rough times they would face in the new enterprise. Each child would have to cooperate if they were going to make it. Most important, the couple outlined *why* they felt it was important to take the risk, and they explained clearly to their kids the potential long-range rewards as well as short-term sacrifices. They mentioned the possibility of failure, which would also be shared by the family. Either in success or failure, the parents emphasized, they wanted to enter this project as a family unit, or not at all.

The kids were able to understand and accept the challenge, and, as their father had predicted, the family went through a couple of hairy years. One Christmas their financial condition was so grim that neighbors chipped in to provide "Care" packages for the holiday meal and the kids' tree. They faced all of this together, the wife remaining loyal and supportive, and constantly reinforcing the children's belief in their father. She helped them all to think in terms of the long-range goal, rather than the short-term hardships, and they all felt proud that they were contributing. Finally, what the father had anticipated for the company began to materialize, and the family was able to share in the rewards for which they had worked so hard. Their family was stronger than ever, because they'd been able to face enormous risks that demanded courage and perseverance from *all* of them.

An executive family that enjoys an US relationship has a built-in defense against many of the inevitable pitfalls of business leadership. The secret is to recognize the symptoms—and to apply the remedies available through an US.

EXECUTIVE FUTURE CHALLENGES

An US is a dynamic relationship that requires constant conscious effort. The results are worth it! In marriage, too, you get what you pay for!

1. How close are the two of you to an US? Each of you should assess the other in terms of the qualities of a whole ME. Which characteristics should each of you work on in striving for an US relationship?

2. Think of situations in your life together where having had an US relationship could have made a difference to your family. Think of a crisis in your life together. Did you react as an US? Was the experience less shattering because you shared it?

5

Applying the US Relationship

For the aspiring young business executive, the first five years on the job can be regarded as a postgraduate course in self-development. The formal education has provided the tools of the trade; *real* learning will start the first day on the job. Most young executives react to this reality by experiencing ebbing confidence, a sense of their own inadequacy, and fear of being exposed before basic new skills can be learned. At home this tension may be reflected in moodiness and a tendency to withdraw from spouse and children. In the face of this apparent isolation, it is especially important for the couple to have considered at length the objectives toward which their first career experience is leading them, and the constraints they will probably encounter along the way. If they are committed to those objectives, and also prepared for the constraints, it may be possible for them to see a light at the end of the tunnel.

On the other hand, through their ability to communicate openly, a young executive couple may find during this difficult period that they have changed their objectives or that they are not sufficiently committed to top-level management goals to justify the pressures involved. They are then in a position to reevaluate their life program, and to opt for another set of goals and another life strategy. We know one couple with two children who decided after six years in industry that the pressures of corporate management placed too great a strain on them as a family. They left the corporation and bought a farm in Maine. The husband, a laywer, hung out his shingle and began developing a small-town law practice, while the wife and children worked the farm. In the future, they may again reevaluate their goals, and make still another career change. The important thing is that this couple is able to communicate honestly and to perceive the freedom to shift courses—to apply the cybernetic approach to their own marriage.

The Executive Ego Crisis and US

Currently, in most executive marriages we know, it is the husband who is involved in the corporate identity struggle. He is the one who feels threatened by the disparity between his ideal and the real business world. While he is experiencing this ego crisis, he demands more than ever the willing support of his wife and family. At this point his wife's ingenuity and knowledge of her husband's personality are put to the test. Some husbands want soft music and a dry martini, others a quiet dinner away from the children, or just a quiet period for thinking. Whatever his individual need, a sensitive wife in an US relationship should be able to recognize it and work to fulfill it, secure in the knowledge that at another time her husband will welcome the opportunity to reciprocate.

It is just as crucial for the husband in an US to be sensitive to his wife's needs in the relationship. He must be prepared to share the problems from her daily life, to see those problems from her perspective, and to give them full weight—as she does his. While the magnitude of their problems may differ, their importance to the person experiencing them does not. Whether the wife works at home, or in a career outside, the traumas of *her* day should not be treated as trivial by her executive husband. An US relationship can make a husband a more sensitive person, both in the family, and in his outside relationships.

Because of our acculturation, which stresses competence and

the ability to cope as specifically male attributes, the unaccus-
tomed pressures of adjusting to an executive career may represent
a particularly harsh ego threat to a man. Until very recently our
culture has discouraged men from openly exposing their insecurities or voicing fear and apprehension. Admitting inadequacies has
been traditionally considered unmanly, a character flaw. Open
communication and free acceptance of an US relationship should
provide a comforting atmosphere in which fear and anxiety can be
expressed.

Frank communication also helps the wife to know that her
husband's irritability and moodiness are not directed at her. She is
better able to accept his behavior, and to recognize it as a transitory phenomenon if she knows that she is not the cause. If she is a
whole ME, she will be able to recognize and accept his need at this
time. This is her time to give, and to build fences to protect the
US. The wife can also take comfort in the knowledge that as her
husband achieves his professional goals and assumes the leadership role he seeks, his own self-image will become more secure.
Gradually it will become easier for him to tolerate the burdens of
executive responsibility in his professional life and to lend confidence and stability to those who work with him. At home he will
find greater ease in merging his own ego into the US, and in sensing
and responding freely to his wife's needs, as she has done to his.

Increasingly, as women assume leadership roles in careers
outside the home, they experience ego-threatening adjustments.
They, too, require the psychological support that can be offered by
another whole ME—in this case the husband in an US relationship.
The test for two whole MEs becomes more important when *both*
partners have demanding leadership roles.

Another threat to the ego of the executive of either sex is both
constant and insidious. This is the danger of jumping—or being
pushed—into a position where he or she cannot perform most
effectively. Characterized Popularly as the "Peter Principle," this
dangerous pitfall can more readily be recognized and avoided by
an executive who is a partner in an US. For example, a male
executive who can admit to his wife, without fear of rejection,
what he perceives as his shortcomings and limitations can see more
clearly both the merits and risks of possible promotions in terms of

his own abilities. A wife who understands her husband's strengths and weaknesses can reinforce his confidence in his real abilities, while supporting his decision not to expose himself to the dangers of an unwise move just for the sake of an apparent promotion.

We watched one family suffer because the husband could not be candid about his own abilities, either to himself or his wife, and because she, in turn, failed to read the real message behind his words. He was extremely successful as a salesman, outselling all the other representatives in his area. His success was recognized, and he was moved into larger and more important sales territories. During all these lateral moves he inflated his own sense of importance by describing to his wife the incompetence of corporate management and by exaggerating his personal contribution to the company's success.

She took his comments at face value and became convinced not only of his importance to the company, but also of his management potential. She urged him to seek a management position, failing to see that his boasting was simply a means of bracing his own ego. She kept pushing him to move up in the corporate structure, and when the job of district manager for the company's largest territory opened up, she prodded him to go after it. He was given a chance to interview for the job, and he was terrified. He finally had to acknowledge to himself that his one talent was for selling, not management. He knew he couldn't handle the job, but he had talked himself into a corner—he either had to show up for the interview or level with his wife. He chose to face the interview, and he deliberately blew his chances. He didn't get the job, and his wife learned for the first time what he really could do—and wanted to do—in the company. Unfortunately the exposure was disastrous for the husband. He could not regain confidence in his ability to sell, and with his very real talent undermined, he went into a slide from which he couldn't recover. The marriage—and both partners —were damaged by their inability to open up to one another.

Merging of Egos in an US Relationship

To create a marriage in which snyergy can occur—where the union can be bigger than the parts that comprise it—individual egos must merge. In an US there is no sovereignty of self. At the beginning of a marriage, both newlyweds may resist relinquishing sovereignty to be part of an US, but the reciprocal benefits soon become obvious.

The ability to focus away from self is especially critical in times of trauma, where it is the survival of the family that's at stake as well as that of an individual within the family. In an ongoing US relationship, personhood is taken for granted, so there's no need to defend it when the going gets tough! Since it's unnecessary to jockey for position within the marriage, self-assertion would be meaningless anyway. But let us repeat, this kind of relationship can only work when a couple is developing into two whole MEs! Further, *each* of those MEs must be consciously working to achieve and preserve the relationship. If only one partner considers the effort worthwhile, it can never really work.

Now, we'll go out on a limb by suggesting that in relinquishing the insistence on self, women—especially women who are mothers—have a cultural advantage over their male partners. In nurturing and caring for children, the sick, and the elderly—traditional female roles in our civilization—many women have learned the importance of substituting gratification of another's needs for immediate gratification of their own. This learned response can often help a wife contribute a little more freely to an US, and can give her a perspective from which to encourage her husband in the wholehearted giving essential to the relationship.

Husbands who have been raised to regard women as persons first, and only secondarily as female persons, may have an easier time in opening up to their wives, and in merging egos in a composite US. While we loudly applaud contemporary recognition that women are not limited to the roles of wife and mother, we also feel encouraged that modern women have unconsciously and automatically gained benefits from their traditional roles: they have a distinct advantage in forming US relationships!

One of the problems experienced by many, if not most, men raised in our society is the difficulty of accepting criticism, especially from women who are close to them. Somehow a whole cultural resistance comes into play, and the possible validity of the critic's remark is lost in the resentment of *her* for making it. One of the advantages of a consciously nurtured US relationship is the security both partners gain in giving *and* receiving criticism. While it may still hurt, and even raise an occasional macho hackle, in a working US a husband has a rationale for evaluating and accepting criticism from his partner.

One of the attitudinal hurdles to be jumped in building an US involves the fear of losing one's individuality. In creating an US, each partner reinforces the other's individuality. We've turned this into a series of "how to" steps. At each step, *discipline* is the key factor.

Step 1 is for each of you to bolster the other's ego through frequent expressions of love and support. In loving one another physically and emotionally, you will be assuring one another of the special qualities that make each of you a unique and valued personality. Each of you is a special human being whose individual quirks and attributes are both recognized and appreciated. Husbands, pay attention! Telling your wife that you love her will never bore her, even if you do it every day. If the words don't come naturally to you, tell her in other ways, but as long as you *sincerely* feel it, show it. Wives, please note: Let your husband know that you appreciate him for his kindness and understanding. Let him know in every way you can how much it means to share his life.

In a real US, spontaneous and mutual expressions of love can emerge in many ways that are meaningful only to you as a symbol of your special shared life. Sometimes such expressions emerge from a tragedy that you've survived together, as well as from the joys you've shared. Because when you have experienced real adversity you can appreciate fully what happiness is!

Step 2 will follow as this totality of feeling is more freely given and accepted, and as the mutuality of your appreciation becomes deeper. Each individual ME will become more secure about being a worthwhile, lovable person with something vital to offer to the other ME.

Step 3 will progress logically from the first two, as each ME almost automatically gives a part of himself or herself to the partner, without sacrificing any real identity. The act of giving itself will produce a feeling of self-worth, as will your partner's acceptance of the giving. As each of you responds to the other's needs, your giving will be rewarded doubly: by your knowledge that you are the only person who can truly sense and fulfill your partner's needs, and by your realization of your own specialness to your partner.

The kind of mutual giving and receiving of love and reinforcement that makes you an US can become a vital part of your nurturing of children. The celebration of self through others that has been characterized as mother love can just as well be father love and children's love once its nature is understood. Real love is a form of *discipline* that teaches us to place others before self.

Many serious students of contemporary society are looking one step beyond the current women's movement and its insistence on nonsexist personhood. They believe, as we do, that once women have successfully established their right to be full-fledged persons, we will all be free to perceive the basic differences between male and female thought processes. It is the fusing of these distinctive thought patterns, arising from evolutionary adaptation and *not* cultural dogma, that can permit the most creative kind of thinking. In this book we emphasize the relationships that can exploit the unique intellectual facilities of both male and female partners.

One executive husband started simply by using his wife as a sounding board to clarify his own ideas. He found that her contributions to his thinking were increasingly important, helping him to make better business decisions. She had educated herself in his professional sphere, and her insights into his business, both intuitive and based on problem solving experience in her own different career area, helped him to resolve problems. If her ideas sometimes bombed—well, his might have been worse, so there was no room for blame.

Naturally, with the realities of classified material and confidential communications, not all career problems can be discussed at home. And in a busy family, there is more to discuss than business decisions. One of the potential strengths of an executive marriage is knowing that both partners can share perspectives on the problems one of them faces. Just as the husband should take advantage of his wife's insights, so the wife should feel free to seek her husband's different training and point of view in dealing with her career problems—whether her career is outside the home, or as a professional wife and mother. Her ideas can provide a fresh perspective within which to consider his work; he can provide a new way for her to perceive her situation.

We contend that cooperation and blending of perspective to solve problems will cease to be a luxury for leadership families but will become a necessity as the pressures to be informed in a wide variety of social areas become too great for one individual.

Obviously, in an US relationship where both partners have become generous, giving MEs, unthreatened by one another, credit for ideas and help will be freely and warmly acknowledged. Unstinting praise, coupled with constructive criticism, can stimulate both partners to greater interest and participation in the other's career and interests. And what works for the marriage partners can also work with children. While their ideas may lack the practicality and wisdom of experience, their fresh perspective and their interest can be invaluable.

Decision Making in an US Relationship

Just as other family hierarchies change over time, so does the hierarchy of decision making. When a young potential executive couple decides on the best graduate school, whether or not to purchase an automobile, or whether to begin a family while still in school, certain rules apply. While both members will contribute to the decision, chances are that more weight will be given to the opinions of the spouse who will be more directly affected by the outcome of the decision: the prospective graduate student; the partner who must commute the greater distance to work; the parent who will have major responsibility for child care.

Throughout the life of the family, *most* decisions will be at least openly discussed, if not arrived at by mutual consent. In an executive family there comes a time when a new element must be considered: the executive's responsibility to his or her corporation, or to the advancement of his or her career, may outweigh the personal preferences and convenience of all family members. This is a true executive dilemma. In such situations, open discussion and consideration of alternatives may still occur, but at some point

interesting choice of words!

the executive (or other leader) is forced to act in the capacity of head of household, and to articulate the overriding claims made by management obligations.

While the concept of a single "head of household" may raise your hackles if you are striving for an egalitarian marriage, we've seen over the years that at some point most executive families have to face up to this situation. Whether or not we use the term, you'll have to deal with the reality. Usually, the decision won't reflect ego dominance, but simply a recognition that many family decisions are made as a direct result of corporate pressures. When the head of your household acts as decision maker, frequently he or she will actually represent family consensus, and clearly this is the ideal situation. But often it is going to be difficult to achieve consensus, especially when children are involved.

When conflicts of interest and desires do occur, and when the executive's career goals must take precedence, it is especially important for your whole family to be able to communicate, and for *all* members to understand as fully as they are able the long-range plans that are involved. Even when they can't agree, it is important for children, in particular, to know that they are not being dismissed or ignored. Any time a career change creates a problem for your children, you should take the time to explain the reasons for the change. The children may not accept the change happily, but will at least realize that their feelings have been considered.

The career influence on a family's decision making is just one more reason why it will be important for your family to reexamine and reevaluate lifetime goals. Your US can be viable only when it is dynamic: nothing is more deadly to a marriage and a family than static interpersonal relationships. Each person in an US should be vibrant and growing. This growth may well result in changing goal orientations, and such changes must be discussed. If one member's motivations and interests change, perhaps your overall career direction will change as well.

We've been close to one couple whose directions and emphasis have altered in response to their growth, and their accommodation to one another has been a joy to watch. As newlyweds they pursued their separate careers. The husband had already established himself in the academic community and was carving out a

distinguished career in research and teaching. The wife finished
her education and entered the legal profession, in which she became increasingly prominent. The husband's research and respected publications added to his distinguished reputation, and he
was regularly wooed by other major universities and by industry.
Each offer was declined because it would involve their relocating.

The couple had continued on this path for some twenty years
when a crisis occurred between the husband and the new administration of his university. While he could continue to teach there,
the situation had become unpleasant for him. As the circumstances
became known in the academic community, he received outstanding offers from several first-rate institutions. She urged him to accept a new position. She gave up *her* options, and encouraged her
husband to make the move—it was her turn to give, and his to
take. Now, after thirty-five years together, this couple is enjoying
a new life in a different community, still secure in their dynamic
and rewarding US relationship.

In our stress-filled society it is more important than ever
before to keep all of our options open. In executive families,
particularly, there must be the freedom to opt out—to choose
deliberately *not* to continue striving for a leadership role, with
attendant corporate pressures and demands on family. In an US
relationship, where open expression is taken for granted, it is much
easier to reformulate goals and redirect the family's life to achieve
greater fulfillment.

The Critic's Role in an US Relationship

As you move upward on the executive ladder, one aspect of your
US relationship will become increasingly important. That is the
ability to give and accept criticism without lasting hurt or recriminations. As one executive wife puts it, "If you're a top banana—
an executive officer or president of your own corporation, president of a university, or President of the United States—you're
going to have a problem. Nobody is going to tell you the real truth
—except your spouse." Everyone enjoys criticizing a leader, but
almost invariably behind his or her back. The willingness to criti-

cize openly—and constructively—is a gift you can give one another in an US relationship. No one will have a better perspective
on the leader's personality, performance, and adherence to principles, and no one will have as good an opportunity to comment
when problems seem imminent.

We have seen it happen again and again as it did to this young
executive. Early in his career, with little preparation for the role,
he inherited an important managerial position. Lacking the psychological readiness, he succumbed to the thrill of his instant promotion with all the brass of a "Lt. Shiny New Bars." In throwing his
weight around, the young executive was particularly obnoxious to
his secretary. She tolerated his swelled head for several months,
and then confronted him. As he was informed, she had been in the
company for many years, and had survived several bosses in his
position. Certainly he had important responsibilities, but she had a
job to do as well, and it was also important. In fact, the company
continued to function because every person in it, from the janitor
to the president, had an important job and did it. Her boss's high-
handed attitude was impairing her ability to do her job effectively,
and she was very willing to take her proven talents to another
position in the company where she could work more comfortably.

Even in his advanced state of ego involvement, the young
executive recognized that his secretary's knowledge of detail and
continuity were indispensable, so he swallowed his rage and asked
her not to transfer. He went home that night seething, expecting
his wife to appreciate his martyrdom and sympathize with his
plight. Instead he got a more elaborate description of his abomina-
ble behavior which, as it turned out, he had *not* been leaving at the
office. His pompous attitude was inflicted not just on those who
worked with him, but on his wife and children as well. Aware of
the strains of the new job, his wife had held herself in check. Now,
since his behavior was causing problems at work, she laid it on the
line. Not only was his secretary right, but she deserved an apology
for what she'd been through.

All of this was hard for him to take, but the husband was
secure in his wife's love and also in the knowledge that what she
was saying was for his good, and that of the company. The soul-
searching he did then was long overdue, but it made him acutely

aware of how difficult he had been. He was able to go to his secretary with a sincere apology, and a plea never to let him get so far
off base again. Obviously, his ability to accept harsh criticism from
his wife—and her freedom to offer it—came out of a mutual respect and love that we have characterized as an US relationship.
They were good friends, willing to help one another. Friendship is
a very important ingredient in an US relationship.

One important reason for building an US in contemporary
society is the information explosion. We are constantly exposed to
a barrage of new information—and that barrage hits leaders first
and hardest. To cope with this influx of data—to distinguish what
is meaningful from what is junk—a leader needs all the help he or
she can get.

EXECUTIVE FUTURE CHALLENGES

As this chapter suggests, if you succeed in being an US, you'll
approach different life situations—personal and professional—in a
special way. Consider these typical situations and assess your own
probable responses. Are you an US? Do you want to be, and are
you willing to work at it consciously?

1. You've moved to a medium-sized city where the male
member of your couple has become the manager of a discount
department store. You are doing very well, and the store is becoming very profitable. Your success has been noticed, and you have
been offered a promotion that would mean managing a chain of
stores in a large city. Both of you are hesitant about the move,
because you're happy in your present community, and also because you're concerned about your capacity to handle the new
position, both in terms of education and experience. You (wife) are
reluctant to express doubts too strongly for fear of thwarting your
husband in a good opportunity, and earning his resentment. You
(husband) are hesitant to express your fears because you don't
want to earn her contempt. How do you make a decision?

2. You are a young couple both doing well in your careers.
You are much alike in planning carefully for your future. After

three years of marriage you've agreed it's time to have your first baby, and the wife is in the third month of pregnancy. Suddenly you (husband) learn you're going to lose your job because your company is facing bankruptcy. You're having difficulty finding another position, and you're despondent. Although both of you are working at being an US, you're also both very private people for whom it is difficult to communicate about feelings. You (wife) are both excited and scared about your impending motherhood, and you really want support and attention. Can each of you forget your problems and support the other? Who should be the giver and who the taker at this crucial time?

6

The Leadership Family and Information Technology

We know you've felt the *effects,* but have you ever stopped to analyze the unseen influence that's at work in your life and your family's? This influence is summed up in the term *information technology* (IT). And whether you welcome it as the harbinger of the next Golden Age or fear it as a greater threat than either the red menace or the far-right lunatic fringe, you're going to have to concede the importance of information technology.

To begin to assess the impact of IT on the everyday life of virtually every person in this country, we need look no further than its visible symbols: the television set in the corner, the radio in the car, or the ever-present telephone. And however great *their* importance, the television, radio, and telephone represent the merest tip of the IT iceberg. The United States, and much of the rest of the modern world, is on the brink of becoming what some observers refer to as an "information society." Social scientists characterize the information society as an evolutionary step equal in importance to either the Agricultural or the Industrial Revolutions. They define it as a post-industrial society whose production and consumption are devoted in major part to the information industry. And if you'll look around, you can see how close we are to achieving that state.

The information society arose out of the enormous capacity of electronic computers and satellites to gather, transmit, and process data. The ability to possess and manipulate information is the key, and it has extended into every phase of our society including federal, state, and local governments; the mass media (radio, television, films, sound equipment and recordings, newspapers, magazines, and books); the education industry; the health care industry; and a variety of specialties in which information experts advise us on specific matters such as law, finance, and insurance. And the *technological* part of information technology also reaches into our private lives—from our electronic ovens to our pocket calculators to the electronic games our children play. We've all become information junkies!

The Modern Executive in IT Land

One fairly immediate and wide-ranging result of IT is that every one of us living in the United States is constantly—and often unwittingly—exposed to an information barrage. We Americans are enormously well informed. Whether or not the information thrust upon us is accurate, whether it is relevant to our needs, and whether we assimilate and use it are all issues beside the point: the information is *there,* and it is virtually inescapable.

For an executive, IT is much more than just a phenomenon to be observed. To succeed in the corporate world the executive must be sensitive to all the influences of IT and must understand information tools and use them effectively. Increasingly, leadership status in any institution will be achieved only by those who are especially adept at making IT work for them. A few of the areas in which IT offers new opportunities for creative management are planning and budgeting, forecasting, inventory control, personnel utilization, and all types of decision making. Information technology has opened whole new industries, and has made possible more rewarding and interesting occupations for non-management employees. But it also brings new dangers to the unwary executive. New sophistication is required to select what is useful and relevant from the total mass of available information. Discriminating information from the data mass becomes an essential art. It can be expressed as follows:

$$D - N = I$$

DATA MINUS NOISE EQUALS INFORMATION!

In seeking and acting on information, an executive must constantly guard against noise, including distorted data, wrong data, and data presented out of context. A special danger facing leaders is a kind of wish fulfillment that could cloud their discriminatory abilities, leading them to perceive as correct those data they wish fervently to believe. It takes a lot of experience and constant attention to assess accurately and quickly what is meaningless noise, and what is really pertinent data. Information discrimination has become a life-long learning process that must be refined constantly in response to new IT tools that themselves compound the information explosion.

Time compression is once again a key factor in the executive's situation. More information is available faster than ever before, so that the task of staying ahead is increasingly difficult. At the same time, the pressure for instant decisions ("tomorrow is too late") can force an executive to act on faulty or prejudicial information. The success of the executive could well depend upon his or her ability to make good decisions. And the quality of the decisions could depend upon the ability to evaluate and use the available information. Therefore, information discrimination can be perceived as one possible key to success for a business executive, or for leaders in academic, religious, or government institutions.

We recently saw a typical example of this when a young executive we know was suddenly bombarded with serious complaints about an operation for which he had responsibility. To deal with the problem he amassed an enormous amount of data. With the added time pressures of this problem on top of his myriad other responsibilities, he reached a decision that was both immediate and drastic. Since we know the young man well, we also have his wife's perspective on the situation. When he arrived home from the office after making his decision, he was still preoccupied with his problem, and she urged him to talk about it. When he'd described his concern in detail, she asked him if he hadn't finally reached his decision on the basis of rather lopsided information.

He realized that in the midst of pressure to do *something* he had, in effect, accepted without question some badly distorted data inputs.

When he returned to his office and sifted carefully through the information he'd digested quickly, he was able to gain a more accurate perspective on his problem, and to reach a far more satisfactory solution. He could have made a serious error in judgment as a result of acting on his assimilation and wrong interpretation of inappropriate data. Whether his error had been prompted by an honest oversight, carelessness, or someone's deliberate manipulation of the data given him, the results would have been the same. An executive must constantly be alert to skewed data inputs.

The magnitude of the problem of information distortion and the importance of information discrimination have been brought home to all of us in our recent political history. One of the young men convicted as a participant in the Watergate incident made an interesting comment when he was interviewed about the matter on television. He said that he was so overwhelmed with the group of people with whom he was working, and so engulfed in their ideas, that he just assumed that what he was doing was proper. He was surrounded by publicly recognized leaders who were positive that what they did was right. He soon forgot even to question the legality, morality, or ethical propriety of their decisions and actions, and his own.

If this young man had learned to debug the inputs he received and to separate the data from the mass of noise, he might possibly have avoided the errors in judgment that led to his conviction and a short prison term. Today, as he lectures on college campuses, he urges students not to shun leadership positions in government, but rather to train themselves to be sharply attuned to the data bombardment that is a part of such positions. He urges them to learn early to weigh information against their *own values,* and to consider their decisions and actions in terms of their personal values and goals, their family's interests and goals, and then the community and nation. He has demonstrated in his own life that in a time of social transition and confusion, such vigilance is imperative for people in leadership positions.

IT and the Executive Family: What You Get Is What You See—and Hear

As a business executive you will not be an isolated individual. You will be a member of a family, and the influences you feel will also affect your family. Information technology is no exception. For you, as an executive, IT will create both new opportunities *and* new problems. And for your family it will offer a mixed blessing of unprecedented avenues for communicating with the world and living conveniently, coupled with the painful necessity of building barriers against unwanted and even harmful information inputs. To enjoy the benefits of IT while withstanding its dangers, your executive family must learn to use information tools effectively, and must be diligent in constructing filters against useless data.

To illustrate the importance of learning this lesson, we'll use the example of a family we know well. The executive husband/ father retired from industry and moved his family from a large city to a smaller university community. Because he had been very prominent in his professional career, his arrival in the new community attracted considerable attention, including some unwelcome publicity in the underground campus paper. This paper published some highly unflattering, even vicious, attacks on the former executive, questioning his business ethics and personal character. These slurs were especially painful to the man's son, a sensitive and troubled teenager. New acquaintances who had read the article teased the boy about it and ridiculed his father. His parents' reassurance that the accusations made in the article were unfounded, and that the attacks were both unscrupulous and untrue, didn't alleviate his shock and hurt. His parents explained that they could not dignify the attacks with a published denial, and tried to help him understand what was happening to them, but the shock he experienced was both severe and impossible to dispel. When, several years later, the journalist responsible for the attacks apologized to the father and admitted that he hadn't investigated the sources of his "facts," the damage to the teenaged son couldn't be undone. The tragedy in this case suggests the terrible dangers of IT: both in the harm that can be done by carelessly neglecting to filter noise from data and thus disseminating distorted information, and in the constant threat to privacy that causes so much pain to leadership families in all fields.

This specific attack on one business leader is typical of what the television medium does all too routinely to the whole business community. Try to think of a situation comedy or mystery drama that doesn't have as butt or villain a character described as a businessman. Rarely is a television hero portrayed as a responsible business leader. Children and other members of the viewing public have little opportunity to identify with a positive role model from the world of business.

One price of leadership, then—not just for the leader, but for his or her family as well—is the effort involved in learning to use IT effectively, and to guard against its often oversimplified messages. In our own experience, we have found that it is usually the wife in an executive family who assumes major responsibility for dealing with IT in the home. She has an unusually good opportunity to become one of the literate minority of people who can use, fully and consciously, the many avenues IT offers for a more vital and enriching existence.

Even without the easily predictable futuristic applications of IT, with a computer terminal becoming as commonplace in many homes as an electric typewriter or a cassette recorder, every family has immediate access to many information tools. One of the most powerful—and overlooked—information filtering devices, for example, is the telephone. This tool is so familiar that the informational implications of its many uses are often ignored. One important information technique that is easily practiced in the home, one that is enhanced by the telephone, is verifying the accuracy of data inputs. A simple but very important use of the telephone for data verification involves communication between the executive spouse and executive secretary. A simple telephone call to compare calendar notes and to confirm the executive's memory of scheduled appointments can avoid a multitude of problems and incredible trauma—such as missed speaking engagements, unexpected dinner guests, and the necessity to be two places at once!

The uses of IT tools in the home aren't exclusively negative by any means. In managing the family's personal finances, insurance, taxes, real estate, and investments, one or the other marriage partner—often the executive wife—must make use of all the tools available to ensure the wisdom of decisions. Using the example of one professional wife who does handle the family investment portfolio, inputs from brokers and other sources are never accepted as the final word. Not only does this investor actively use the telephone to review alternate sources of information, but she also takes advantage of independent research tools, including several data banks accessible to her. She is as thorough and systematic about the complexities of this aspect of her career as her husband is about any of the areas of *his* professional competence, and just as sophisticated about the use of IT tools.

In addition to using information tools to verify accuracy of data brought into the home, parents—especially those whose careers keep them in the home—have both an opportunity and a responsibility to sensitize themselves to the diverse impacts of IT on every member of the family. We believe that the best filter a family can construct against inadvertent and potentially harmful information impacts is an outgrowth of an US relationship: a husband and wife "fence." When a couple and their children build a mutual framework for relating to one another and to the outside world, they automatically build a bulwark of security against any informational onslaught. Whether the noise takes the form of helpful criticism, such as we've described earlier, or comes through sophisticated media presentations that glorify values or lifestyles contrary to the family's standards, an US relationship can provide a protective shell within which those threats can be handled.

The potential harm of encroaching information inputs shouldn't be minimized; they can be threatening even to adults, but are potentially most unsettling to children who are suddenly exposed to ideas, standards, and behavior dramatically different from what they have experienced at home. While there is no way for even the most diligent parent to isolate a child from these influences in our information-oriented world, a good measure of protection can be offered by parents who instill and constantly reinforce their own standards. Such parents can provide the security blanket of an US relationship for a frightened and bewildered child to fall back on. Other parents who are not so lucky and do not have this kind of central stability can become victims of their children's unhappiness and their own inability to cope with it. This sometimes seriously undermines the marriage itself. Such parents often succumb to blaming one another for the situation, and for the incomprehensible behavior of their children. The once happy home becomes intolerable for one or both partners, and such dissatisfaction often leads to separation and divorce.

In building an information filter for your family, an important ingredient is constant awareness of what's going on with one another. Both you and your children should be sensitive to and willing to discuss the outside information influences on your family, especially when these involve confusing or frightening conflicts with your family's ideals and beliefs. As parents you may be utterly bewildered in trying to counteract what may be the most popular information medium for your kids—contemporary music, as it is packaged and distributed by the super-powerful recording industry.

During the peak of the acid rock era we shared the agony of one executive family as they became totally confused by their teenager's change of attitude toward them. As a close-knit family they had always enjoyed one another. The parents had consciously lived by the principles they advocated, and felt they could counter outside influences by setting a good example at home. They were not hypocritical, they believed in the soundness of their values, and they frankly couldn't understand their young son's growing hostility toward them. Increasingly the boy closeted himself in his room, wearing his earphones, and lost himself in his record and tape collection. Desperate to reach him *some* way, the mother finally began paying attention to the music—and the *words*—her son was hooked on. She discovered too late the vicious attacks to which the family's middle class morality and commitment to the American system were being subjected. Worst of all, she had no effective information medium for responding to and rebutting the attacks. Like most parents, she and her husband had failed to grasp the pervasiveness of media influences on their own child.

It's hard for an adult to accept that kids can become so saturated with what they hear on radio, records, and tapes, and what they see in films and on television, that this media world becomes their special reality. They live in what we call a "data reality," and they lack the ability, or even the motivation, to filter out the meaningless noise of that environment. They don't distinguish between *their* data reality, and *our* real-world reality, and a gap develops that we can't fill with all our truth, listening, and understanding. All facts and information are forced into comformity with *their* real world, and what can't be forced to conform isn't considered. If we're painting a frightening picture, that's just what we intend to do. We don't ever want to see other parents face what our friends faced in learning about this informational disparity the hard way.

Because, in part, we want this to be a "how to" book, we're going to offer some suggestions for dealing with the kind of problem we've described. Using our example of contemporary music, we say it isn't sufficient for you as parents just to listen to music your kids play. Even understanding it isn't enough. You must really put yourselves into your children's perspectives, and recognize that most children grow up dissatisfied with an imperfect world, and seeking messages (the more simplistic, the better) about a better way. Kids often find the message of their chosen music (or films, or television) quite legitimate, even though the message deals only with one aspect of reality and obscures or ignores conflicting facts. Taking a readily perceived injustice, sophisticated informational techniques can be employed to distort that undeniable reality until it becomes an enormous flaw of the entire social system, and only radical solutions can offer hope of change.

Young people today are particularly receptive to persons we describe as "critics in residence." These people are convincingly expert in pointing out inadequacies and deficiencies in our society. At the same time, they effectively are able to avoid responsibility for solving the problems they so dramatically expose. Today, there are countless interest groups that are particularly attractive to sensitive, idealistic young people. As was mentioned previously, many of our lyrical balladeers use their music to expose a variety of societal ills. Since there is no need to observe the many constraints that our leaders must in solving society's problems, these "critics in residence" can be convincingly critical of our leaders in all our institutions. Young people who are just starting to become their own persons and who are breaking away from parental dependency are particularly vulnerable and receptive to this kind of persuasion.

Even in adult society the notion of statistical verification of observations gets more lip service than practice, and for kids in their formative years it has no relevance at all. Young children live in a right or wrong world, and when they become adolescents exposed to the sophistications of our emerging information society, they often tend still to see it in black-and-white terms, without the reservations dictated by adult logic. Further, young people have become so accustomed to the instant solutions of television dramas that they have never developed the capacity to see situations through to their conclusion or to work out solutions for difficult problems. If crimes can be solved, diseases cured, and marital conflicts patched up in thirty minutes or an hour on the tube, why should an adolescent expect real-life problems to be any less susceptible of instant fixing? Unfortunately, the tendency to give up on what isn't easy seems to be pervasive in our culture. "It's too tough—leave it" and "it's used—buy a new one" seem to be key phrases in our "disposable" society.

Adolescents are much more prone than adults to accept new impressions with little evaluation of them, and their strong positions on issues can confound their parents who have learned to live in a world characterized by shades of gray.

This is a difficult period for leadership parents. These trying times really test the strength of their US relationships. Both parents should have developed enormous emotional resources to be able to weather this frustrating, adolescent, young adult development period. Humor, again, plays a very special role. No matter how angry or hurt or threatened you may be by the values and attitudes of the emerging adults in your family, this is the time to laugh a lot together. We know that to replace anger with humor is an incredibly difficult task. You will have many failures. One of the best ways to keep the lines of communication open and have a dialogue going between yourself and your children is to *listen* to what they have to say *without interruption*. Nothing destroys a communication faster than a parent interrupting a child when he or she is speaking. Bombarded by IT inputs, adolescents are particularly vulnerable. They are constantly wrestling with all kinds of ideas, trying to sort them out. Listen to your children with an open and receptive mind. You do not have to agree with their ideas but give them the courtesy of hearing them without interruption. Possibly, your children may be right. When that is the case, let them know immediately that you have changed your thinking. Do not wait. There is no greater ego boost for your kids than to know that you think their ideas have substance.

If you have not changed your mind, treat the differences between you with humor, patience, and love. If you fail in this most difficult process, do not become depressed or discouraged. It may be years before your attitudes and values are understood by your children. Just recently, a very happy mother related this experience she had with her daughter. The daughter had emerged from being a troubled teenager. At the age of thirty-two she had grown into a mature responsible adult. The years in between had been full of heartbreak and trauma for her parents. When she found herself, she sent her mother a beautiful letter thanking her for her patience and understanding. Unfortunately, not all parents will receive such tangible reinforcement.

The mutual frustration of parent and child is inevitable in every family, but it can become impossible in a family where there is no awareness or preparation. We say: recognize that it will happen to *you* and try to stay close enough to your children and their experiences (both actual ones, and those gained through their data reality) to maintain communication.

Your adult world is going to get more confusing, with new and unexpected time compression and IT pressures, and the world your children are experiencing will be chaotic beyond anything our generation or yours has experienced. Keep talking to your kids!! Keep talking to one another! Have an US relationship that is solid enough to offer you stability and solace, and that allows you to define and present a united front in dealing with your children and their media world. Maybe your kids won't turn out as you'd wish. But at least you'll be together, and you won't fall into the all-too-common trap of blaming one another for your "failure" in raising your kids. Awful as it is to say, sometimes children are unhappy and unreachable no matter what. In an executive family where the pressures are greater, the chances for unhappiness are also greater.

If it should happen to you, don't let your marriage be a victim of circumstances. The stronger you are, the stronger your US, the better the chance your children have of surviving the changing pressures of growing up in an Information Society.

A final "how to" on the subject is really a "how not to." That is, don't give up on your own values just because they're in conflict with the "now" values. We've watched too many parents lose themselves and one another because they've felt compelled to capitulate in trying to preserve their families. We say you can remain consistent in your own values, and in expressing them, and still love the child. If you and your family are an US, you can retain your own sense of self-respect and still stay close to your children. In an US there's room for "love me, hate my lifestyle!"

Leadership and the Media in an Information Society

Throughout history, transitional periods have been accompanied by upheavals in social institutions, and the family is one of the most vulnerable and one of the first to be attacked. We'd like to go on record as believing that the family is here to stay. Historically, the family has been the mainstay of society; if the family is destroyed, generally all social institutions follow. What distinguishes our present period of social ferment, and the attacks on the family that accompany it, is in part Information Technology. Rejection of traditional family values, youth rebellions, and urban guerillas are all glorified in the media for our children to see and relate to. And as we've said earlier in this chapter, the impact of such media reality on our children cannot be overemphasized. We believe that to counteract this very visible and vocal dissenting minority, leaders and their families have an obligation to be increasingly responsible for their own actions and responsive to the situation in their communites, the nation, and the world.

Leaders in today's IT world have *instant* influence. Their most casual and thoughtless remarks are immediately known throughout the world, just as are their most private social and moral indiscretions. With the other side getting so much press, it is essential that those leaders who do believe in the continuity of the family, in personal ethics that extend into all phases of life, and in the future of our American system not only speak out, but *live* their beliefs. They must be conscious in exploiting the tools of IT—especially the media—rather than letting the media exploit them.

Those leaders who enjoy direct media responsibility have an obligation to exercise some voluntary control over what they project. We believe those obligations go beyond the equal-time provision, and certainly beyond simplistic family-hour programming, and extend to the basic issues of truth, honor, and genuine concern for the potential impact of the messages they convey. And because, in a balanced society, no single institution should act unilaterally, it becomes the responsibility of leaders in every social institution to convey their own attitudes and beliefs about what is appropriate and responsible action for the media and other IT related institutions.

In earlier chapters we discussed the value of an US relationship as a bulwark against the many pressures forced upon leaders and their families. The US is certainly one of the most effective frameworks within which to develop successful techniques for information discrimination. There are, as well, several other effective tools of special value to leadership couples in an Information Society. We describe them as the A-Friend Theory, the Umbrella Theory, and Time Resource Management. They are discussed in the following chapter.

EXECUTIVE FUTURE CHALLENGES

We hope you've begun to see how important the tools of Information Technology will be in your own leadership family. As you read through and consider the following situations, apply IT techniques to your approach to solving them.

1. You are an aggressive and ambitious young business executive, working for a fast-growing company in an exciting industry. Part of your job is gathering, sorting, and channeling data for management reports to the senior executives so that they can make better decisions for the company. There is an enormous amount of data that must be sifted, weighed, and interpreted. Another young executive is doing a job similar to yours. Your information filtering and evaluation has led you to a judgment vastly different from his. Each of you has a different impression of what is data and what is noise, and the company's continued success depends upon the correctness of decisions made on the basis of the report accepted. What do you do?

2. You are the wife of a public figure. Your husband has been the target of criticism by the media. You're particularly disturbed because what they are saying about your husband isn't true, but it is coming to the attention of your three children who range in age from ten to twenty. You desperately want to shield them from the slurs directed against their father. How do you build an effective "fence" to protect them?

Other Tools for Leadership Families

7

In shaping and controlling your own life, it will be necessary for you as a leadership family to develop a variety of tools to help you adapt to the changes you *will* face. The first and most effective, for your inner peace and contentment, is an US relationship. But your leadership family cannot remain inwardly focused, no matter how zealously you may guard your privacy. And so you must develop other tools to help you relate to the world outside your US.

The Leadership Family and the A-Friend Theory

In observing executive marriages over the years, we've seen that one of the sturdiest supports for the US comes from outside the couple. We've formulated our observations into what we call the A-Friend Theory. The A-Friend Theory says that in addition to the spouse in an US relationship, each of us needs at least one A-Friend of our own sex. This is an intimate friend who offers the kind of accepting comradeship that strengthens self-confidence and reinforces individual security.

67

Ideally, in an US relationship, husband and wife are in effect one another's A-Friends of the opposite sex, sharing not only the intimacies of marriage and family life, but also the rewards of solid, noncompetitive, and intellectually stimulating *friendship*. This special relationship within the marriage is reinforced by each partner's A-Friendships outside.

An A-Friend of the same sex fulfills a different and very important role. In sharing one's biological (and often one's culturally ingrained) point of view, this A-Friend can provide a secondary filter for evaluating both new information and one's attitudes toward it.

Although the relationship hasn't been identified in our terms, A-Friendships often occur between siblings or between parents and children in close-knit families. The A-Friendship has traditionally been the heart of the television situation comedy. The entertainment media have long capitalized on this relationship.

Once again, for an executive or other leadership family, the situation is "the same only more so." For the wife of an executive, a woman A-Friend can relieve the burdens of loneliness and frustration that trouble even the closest of US relationships, particularly when prolonged separations or other leadership traumas occur; she can share "woman talk," and can provide a break from the boredom and weariness of homemaking and mothering.

An especially important role of an A-Friend can be to furnish an outlet for pent-up frustrations. Even in the most carefully planned and openly discussed executive marriages, resentments are bound to occur over the seemingly endless sacrifices one spouse can be called on to make. In two-career marriages (discussed more fully in a later chapter), interruptions to the growth of one career may cause resentment, even though the agreement to make the other career primary has been reached voluntarily. A

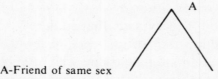

A-Friend of same sex   A-Friend of opposite sex
                                               (Partner in an US relationship)

spouse caught in this situation needs to express feelings of disappointment and rage. A sympathetic A-Friend, who has no personal involvement in the conflict, can absorb the verbal abuse, keeping a lot of negative and potentially guilt-producing emotion out of the marriage.

One of the biggest hazards and often one of the greatest strains on an executive marriage is mobility. Uprooting and moving families not only to other cities, but even to different countries, has proven to be a hardship for many families. In our own corporate lives, we've seen how a professional executive wife can be of enormous help to other executive families by becoming a temporary A-Friend to the wives whose husbands have been relocated by the corporation. Often a kind and understanding executive wife can offer her own stability and can share her experiences and insights with families who may be new to the organization or the area. Active feminists may deplore this mothering role, but we've watched it help turn around what could have been a lonely and miserable period of transition for many young wives. Here again, we see IT in its simplest form—the spoken word and an act of kindness—affecting attitudes and directing the approach to a problem, in this case executive mobility, into a positive frame of reference.

In multinational oil companies, where hardship posts are a commonplace, corporate housing is often arranged to facilitate A-Friend relationships. A young executive family, transferred in midwinter to an oil post in the North Sea, has few sources of comfort. But one salvation is that the family will be housed among a number of other such families, a built-in source of A-Friends who are in identical circumstances. When a child becomes ill or a mother depressed, someone who understands what is needed is available to step in and help! It's normal to gripe. An A-Friend to gripe to —one who gripes back, but who can still perceive the humor in the shared predicament—can mean the difference between despair and making it!

Today's young people have recognized the importance of the telephone as a tool for helping one another in times of trouble as the crisis lines and hot lines in virtually every city will attest. In executive families this technological tool has been the salvation of many a young wife and mother who feels lost and helpless in a new environment.

As a family who benefitted from her ministrations, we'll never forget one boss's wife whose timely calls just to check up or to suggest a new playground or activity for the kids really saved us. When we were lonely and on the verge of terminal self-pity, her phone calls really helped change our attitude toward our relocation to a new city.

For executives enmeshed in all the problems and pressures of highly complex careers an A-Friend of the same sex can sometimes offer new perspectives on a personal situation and insights into the intricacies of other professions. For a young manager who is threatened by feelings of inadequacy, compounded by ordinary job frustrations, an A-Friend can offer reassurance and a diversion. The friend may be in the same profession (not usually in the same company, because job competition can put strains on any friendship), and can act as another sounding board for complaints and far-out ideas that can't be aired to colleagues. The perceptions this friend can offer, and perhaps the commonality of professional pressures, is a resource that is different from that provided by the executive's spouse, the opposite-sex A-Friend. Being able to unload anxieties and try out ideas on a knowledgeable and trusted friend may help the young executive to gain reassurance or may help to point out flaws in his or her thinking. Ideally, for both marriage partners the A-Friend relationships outside the marriage should strengthen the US relationship within it, reinforcing the importance of each ME as a respected and loved individual.

When either the husband or the wife chooses an A-Friend of the opposite sex outside the marriage, things can get sticky. This happens fairly often in open marriages, and in our opinion is one good argument against such marriages, which too often end in separation and divorce. The cliché office marriage, in which the secretary becomes the executive/husband's A-Friend, and shares both his working day and the intimacies of sex, can be a disaster for a marriage. Here again, an US relationship between husband and wife is the strongest bulwark against divisive outside relationships.

Children are sometimes quicker than adults to perceive the value of friendships. Many an adolescent has survived the pain of growing up because of the security and reinforcement provided by a best friend who is sharing the trauma. In contemporary society, many of us pay psychiatrists or other mental health therapists to act in the capacity of A-Friends, listening sympathetically to our problems, and helping us to filter information. Even though the therapist is paid to listen, the patient may be able to identify with him or her and to use the professional relationship as a temporary surrogate for a spontaneous friendship. And that brings us to a final point. It's possible to act as an A-Friend in an essentially one-sided relationship. Often we can either *be* a good listener, or use a good listener, without entering into a reciprocal relationship. If the relationship answers the need of providing a vehicle for expressing and gaining insights into one's problems and ideas, then it serves the purpose of an A-Friendship for the individual at that particular time in his or her life.

Staying on Course:
Seeing-Eye Friends

In keeping on track, it is essential for a leader to have access to another trusted point of view—a spouse who is an A-Friend and an A-Friend of the same sex. They can both help to reinforce an executive's perspective or to identify blind spots that might prevent him or her from perceiving a situation clearly. No one is lonelier than a leader struggling with an ethical question, and at no time is it more important for a husband and wife to have an US relationship, and for *both* to have A-Friends outside the marriage. Both kinds of A-Friends are important not only as sounding boards for help in unscrambling the issues, but also as a source of honest moral reinforcement—a kind of ethical security blanket. A spouse who offers love and support, who understands and accepts the leader's concern and dedication, can question and examine concepts and positions without threatening or appearing to challenge the leader's integrity or ability. Most important, the knowledge that there will be no rejection or moral hindsight if the *wrong* decision is made can give the leader the courage to act to the best of present knowledge and ability, and later to acknowledge and attempt to rectify errors. "I'm with you 100%," can be very sweet words when difficult decisions must be made, and the people from whom those words mean the most are the A-Friends.

A sensitive spouse and another honest and concerned A-Friend can sometimes help an executive to gain insights into corporate tendencies. Sometimes spotting potentially dangerous trends before they really develop can give an executive a valuable opportunity to ward off future ethical, or even legal, conflicts by anticipating them and acting *now* to forestall dangerous developments. An A-Friend who is attuned to the leader, one who is used as a sounding board for his or her problems, can often help to generate alternatives and to prevent crises.

The Leadership Family and the Umbrella Theory

The Umbrella Theory was evolved from our observations of leadership families in our information oriented world. People—especially leaders—need a way to handle inputs that conflict with their own perceptions and values without either rejecting the people who hold these conflicting ideas *or* changing personal values to agree with the new ones. The Umbrella Theory is a tool for dealing with different social values in a calm and undisturbed manner. It's the "Umbrella Theory" because it's all encompassing.

First, the Umbrella Theory says, there is no dramatic change in basic social values. There *are* new attitudes expressed by some individuals. This means that we are all exposed to such new attitudes, and we can then either relate them to our own lives or ignore them. But we don't have to reject the people who express those attitudes, any more than we have to accept the attitudes themselves just because we know about them. That's so simple that we're almost embarrassed to call it a theory—and yet how many times have we all seen uptight people who refuse to talk to those they label as "oddballs." Then there is the opposite: middle-aged adolescents who feel compelled to adopt the latest youth-spawned craze they've discovered. The Umbrella Theory simply says, "I can know you and like you, but I sure don't have to do or think what you do and think." It's just that basic. And if we could just remember to apply the Umbrella Theory, and teach our kids to apply it, think of all the grief we'd be saved.

Without question, the information explosion has forced our awareness of many issues and attitudes that now are openly discussed or acknowledged in the public media. Homosexuality, abortion, venereal disease, legalized prostitution, and child abuse are just a few examples of topics that weren't widely discussed in earlier decades, because they were simply suppressed from public view.

To choose intelligently between accepting and rejecting, it's necessary to exercise information discrimination. And, of course, this is another area in which executives and other leaders must be prepared to act in advance of the rest of the population. To deal effectively with the many individuals who will employ, be employed by, and work with him or her during a career, an executive must be prepared to recognize unemotionally the many differences that exist in backgrounds, attitudes, and values. To interact with a variety of people who are useful, contributing members of the corporation, an executive must understand and accept their different approaches to life, even though he or she may have no interest in sharing any of them. In effect, the Umbrella Theory allows the executive to see and enjoy the potential of each person, instead of being stopped short by a color, a shaved head, or a nose ring!

The advantages to society are obvious. In most neighborhoods, the arrival of a black family has ceased to be cause for disturbance, if even for comment. And in industry the number of black people in leadership positions has increased dramatically over the last couple of decades. Having a black person or a woman for a boss today is pretty unremarkable in many corporations, yet fifteen years ago such a situation would have represented a struggle from both the management and employee points of view. Today, more often than not, a person who is competent is judged on the basis of that competency, without respect to color or sex. And in just a few years, we hope that other minorities will have achieved similar breakthroughs.

The distance we've come in the last few years can be per-

ceived in the most liberating of *all* the recent liberation movements
—the one relating to alternate lifestyles. Less than a decade ago
most parents would not admit—*if* they were aware—that their
children might observe a different standard of sexual behavior from
their own, and yet today few mothers hesitate to refer to a child's
roommate of the opposite sex. Similarly, neighborhoods that
would have shunned communal family groups now accept them
somewhat more readily, and their children are welcomed into the
mainstream of child-centered activities.

Fashion, once a true indicator of social position, has similarly
ceased to be a measure of a person's status. The concern with
comformist attire is forgotten in today's business world, even in
the last bastions of conservatism, our banks and other financial
institutions. Both men and women dress to suit their own taste,
and find their appearance readily accepted. We're not extending
this generality to include messy or grotesque dress styles, although
even those are unquestioned in many corporate and other institutional settings. But we can safely say that women no longer feel
uncomfortable in a social or business situation when they don't
wear gloves and hats, and in most corporations the uniform of dark
suit, white shirt, tie, and brief case is observed more as an exception than as the rule. Ironically, the independent executive is now
most often the one who shows up in traditional, rather than trendy
attire. We think the disappearance of rigid dress codes reflects
generally greater tolerance in corporations (and in all of society)
for people who are visibly different. There is still plenty of room
for improvement, but the movement toward relaxation is off to a
strong beginning.

Unfortunately, the trend away from rigidity also means confusion, to an extent, in that the executive won't be able to fall back
on time-honored guidelines to direct his or her decisions. Company
policy is changing virtually overnight, reflecting both informal and
formal social changes. The formal changes are represented by laws
being passed at federal, state, and municipal levels that make un-
acceptable what has been totally legitimate corporate behavior.
The most obvious examples relate to color and sex discrimination
in hiring and promotion, but equally dramatic and far-reaching
changes relate to the individual responsibility of corporate officers

and board members for the policies of their companies. And, by the way, the legal culpability of board members adds both a new dimension of vulnerability *and* a new responsibility to ensure access to accurate and absolutely current information for the protection of the companies as well as of the individual board members.

Going on with our Umbrella Theory, we should point out that social attitudes are subject to time compression. Every one of us is going to be forced into reexamining his or her values almost continuously—to consider new ones, and then either to reject them or to relate them to our personal value systems. There won't be time to cope with all the new ideas about which we are informed, so more than ever it will be essential to have a firm foundation of goals, values, and personal beliefs to provide a framework within which to assess our own and our family's progress. It's going to be necessary to engage in constant value assessment and adjustment. We need neither experiencing culture shock nor surrender when we encounter new and increasingly bizarre values or lifestyles. Another occasion when:

INFORMATION EQUALS DATA MINUS NOISE!

Again, the Umbrella Theory is essential for executives working with people who march to a different drummer. It becomes important for executive families to benefit from exposure to other members of the community whose lives touch theirs. As an example, parents now can relate more objectively to gifted schoolteachers whose style of dress, living arrangements, and sexual orientation differ radically from their own. Parents may be able to accept more readily that such people can instruct their children effectively without necessarily influencing them into new value systems. In order to feel comfortable and unthreatened, the parents must first understand and feel confident with their own values, and which continue to be presented clearly to their children by precept in the family's daily life.

This consideration leads back once more to the vital importance of an US relationship in dealing with both family values and IT inputs. The process of constructing information filters, and making decisions regarding informational inputs, is not a simple one for the individual or for the family. To deal with the complexities of information bombardment, and to choose or reject from among the alternatives available, requires interpersonal communication within a group of mutually sympathetic and committed individuals —a family and a few A-Friends.

In our present transitional society it is difficult to adjust to the fact of change itself, and to cope with individual changes as they occur. Simple right and wrong decisions are seldom that: multi-value systems apply. The emphasis assigned to different values shifts according to the individual's personal criteria. A family that has established communication, and in which it is possible to express confusion and fear, has a better than average chance of producing individuals who can cope with the complexities of our times.

IT and the Great American Guilt

The Jewish mother celebrated in comedy has been embraced as a symbol of universal guilt giving. In our myth, this being has so imbued us with a sense of our own innate wrong-headedness and disloyalty that we accept, or even embrace, guilt for *everything,* from forgetting a birthday through causing the polar ice cap to melt! In fact, much of the guilt we experience as Americans is a result of imperfectly filtered information. We let too much get through to us that should be discarded as meaningless noise.

For example, if an executive father must travel extensively, critics heap guilt on him because his children are suffering without him. If an executive wife chooses to devote her energies to home and family, instead of to an outside career, there is someone to suggest that she is not sufficiently interesting or active for a man of her husband's stature. If a child runs afoul of authorities, it's read as a sure sign of parental neglect.

Each of these barbs can reach home and cause pain, because each individual is constantly faced with complex decision making and value choices: Should the father go on an important business trip, or attend a child's recital? Having weighed his choices and made his best judgment in the face of conflicting data he is, of course, open to criticism for having rejected either argument. The wife and mother feels not only the attractions of pursuing her own career, but also the pressures of the current women's movement, urging her to free herself of the "bonds" of homemaking. If she opts to stay at home as a professional wife, she is ripe for her critics' attacks, but if she goes out to a career, she is abandoning her responsibilities to her children. The guilt of parents about their children is the cruelest of all, because no parent is capable of making right decisions all the time. Each must acknowledge and live with clear mistakes, and is doomed to puzzle over how things "might have turned out if only. . . ."

To compound all this guilt, Information Technology exposes parents to new decision-making pressures, and time compression dictates that there is less time to evaluate data inputs and, concurrently, a greater number of important decisions to be made. For parents there is the added knowledge that the pervasiveness of IT inputs effectively prevents protecting any child once that child is old enough to perceive the world portrayed through the media. We can't obviously, offer answers to this increasingly disturbing problem. We can only share our experience and offer some practical approaches to coping.

First, have an US, both as a framework for teaching children about family values and as a hedge for you as a couple against parental guilt and the inevitable blame and infighting that accompany it. Next, have A-Friends outside yourselves against whom you can bounce ideas and complaints, and through whom it's easier to recognize what is a valid and what is an unreasonable rule to apply to kids. Filter out as much as possible of the meaningless noise that can come in from family, neighbors, and the countless experts who know just how everybody else's kids should be raised. For some kids, the old-fashioned idea of personal responsibility is the best instructional technique: "Go ahead and do it, but you're going to get in trouble for it. And you'd better be able to get yourself out."

Finally, extend the tolerance of the Umbrella Theory both within the family (kids being more tolerant of parents, as well as parents being more accepting of their children) and outside it. Don't judge other people's children, and don't judge other parents by looking at their children. A child who is a brat at ten may be tolerable at fourteen. An impossible teenager may become a charming adult. And adults who condemn others as bad parents frequently find their criticisms coming home to roost when their own model children suddenly turn anti-social and repulsive. When in doubt, remember the advice a friend gave us: "Never judge anyone until that person reaches at least the age of thirty. There have been *great* late bloomers! Just look at Winston Churchill!"

Management of the Time Resource

Among the many ways that leadership families differ from others is in the relation to and use of time. Such families must be among the first to view time as a valuable and irreplaceable resource, because more than any other element of our Information Society leaders are subjected to its rigors. A leadership family simply cannot afford to use time the same way as can less committed families. A problem exists because of the number of external institutions with which leadership families interact.

Because they have assumed a leadership role, family members are generally expected to be active in all aspects of their lives: professional organizations, church groups, political parties, community service clubs—*all* demand blocks of time from leadership families. It becomes imperative for the leadership family to budget time, assigning priorities to various institutions, allowing maximum commitments to some and minimum commitments to others. This ranking of commitments should, of course, reflect the values of the individual and of the family unit.

The proper utilization of the time resource is of critical importance in building a society in which the roles of integral institutions are balanced. That is, leaders must consciously budget and use their time in helping to achieve a society in which development of cultural institutions will keep pace with scientific and technological institutions.

How will all of this affect your own leadership family? For one thing, you will find it necessary to take an active role in community affairs. To a greater extent than ever before, as a business executive, you must have a voice in local, state, and national government, representing the point of view of the responsible business community in affairs of social, cultural, and educational importance. As a business leader of the future you *must* be at the vanguard of change toward bettering the community in which you live. In this way you can work to improve the negative image that has been attached to business. Such involvement will be a major obligation for you as a leader and for your family.

You and other leaders in the emerging society, must use IT tools effectively to gain a global perspective on social, cultural, economic, political, and technological developments. Only such an all-encompassing perspective can lead to a balanced world society. At the present time, such a perspective is extremely difficult to achieve because of IT distortions, such as emphasis on one or only a few institutions, propagandistic repetition of certain inputs, or skewed messages concerning the roles and contributions of institutions. Part of your strength, as a future leader, must lie in your ability to filter out such distortions.

The destructive potential of IT will increase with intensification of time compression, and will ultimately force the creation of a sort of information compression that does not now exist. You and other leaders of the future must cooperate to develop a new conceptual framework through which individuals will be able to deal with time and information compression. Such a framework will probably still be built around personal values and preferences, but because of your special knowledge and perceptions you will be able to introduce an element of conscious striving toward balance of interrrelationships among institutional roles and values.

Separation or compartmentalization of your various institutional roles will become increasingly less possible. To be at the forefront of these exciting developments, the first and essential step will be for you and your family, and other leadership families, to become accomplished at managing and allocating your time resource for maximum effectiveness.

Now that we've explored becoming an US, forming and depending on A-Friend relationships, applying the Umbrella Theory, and managing the time resource, you have been exposed to some of the tools for achieving a well-balanced leadership family. Now let's consider how they might actually be put to work in your family, *if* a well-balanced leadership family is your goal.

EXECUTIVE FUTURE CHALLENGES

Taking into consideration the tools described in this chapter, try to put yourself in the following situations, and see how you might respond.

1. Your company is transferring you (husband) to another city. The move will involve not only a promotion, but also a job situation you've sought for some time. You (wife) are reluctant to leave the community where you now live, and where you have achieved prominence as a leader in your own endeavors. You have a close friend to whom you confide your reluctance and fears. Are you (husband) in a position to offer any help?

2. You are a senior executive in a corporation that has always had the reputation of being extremely conservative in its image. A junior executive of undeniable competence and good prospects for advancement has decided to challenge the company's conservatism by flaunting his alternate lifestyle. This has caused a great deal of scuttlebutt and some polarization among employees. It's now become disruptive to productivity. What do you do?

8

Getting to be a Balanced Leadership Family

We'd like to introduce a new concept in family organization that can be one outgrowth of an US relationship. We call it a "balanced family." As we see it, this balanced family has the inner strength and mutual devotion that characterize an US, *balanced* by a commitment to and active role in other institutions. We believe the ideal of balance between internal and external relationships is especially important in leadership families—and that balanced leadership families can be instrumental in guiding our society toward a balance in all institutions.

Throughout history, the family has been one of the first social institutions to come under attack in periods of turmoil and social transition. The family is a natural target because it lacks a formal protective structure that is common to many other institutions. When its nurturing function is diminished in times of social unrest the family is very vulnerable to attack by those dissatisfied with the status quo and seeking radical solutions.

Evolution of the Family

The majority of the world's adult population, including some forty-eight million adults in the United States, still lives in a conventional family situation based on monogamous marriage. Yet, in the contemporary United States, some serious thinkers are speculating on the possible dissolution of the family as a unifying force. The American emphasis on self-reliance, current movements focusing on the rights of women and children, shifting responsibility for the care of the elderly, and wide acceptability of alternate lifestyles are cited as peculiarly American forces responsible for the present attacks on the family.

We are convinced that current negativism concerning the future of the family is a transitory state. Once the fad passes, the people who persist in proclaiming the death of the family will find themselves out of style. The family has consistently survived attacks and pronouncements of its doom. We say it will last until a better alternative comes along and works as well for the *majority*. Currently, most alternate approaches to adult unions tend to be temporary; longevity is not even considered a positive value in the relationship. Not enough time has elapsed to assess fairly the durability of alternate lifestyles or the social and emotional by-products of serial short-term relationships.

Many like to quote alarming statistics concerning the future of the family, but statistics are prone to manipulation; they tend to reflect the persuasion of the person invoking them. Antagonists of conventional family living arrangements quote figures showing that one out of three marriages ends in divorce. For them, this statistic proves that marriage is no longer viable. For us, that statistic can be inverted to prove that marriage has never been stronger in the United States. At a time when all social institutions are in a state of flux, two out of three marriages endure! Further, a large percentage of those people who have divorced soon remarry, indicating their belief in the institution and eagerness to try again.

We don't argue the validity of many social changes that have contributed to the present precarious state of the family, nor do we propose in any way a return to the good old days of the traditional family. We *do* argue in favor of the evolution of a new family form, geared to contemporary life. Herbert Hendin, a psychoanalyst who has done extensive investigation on the family, says "It is idle to think we can just go back to 30 or 40 years ago. We can't go back. It won't work. We are going to have to look at families with understanding and see what we can do to make family life work in the '70s and '80s." *

Historically, the family in the United States has included a father (undisputed head of household), a mother, and their children. Other relatives—grandparents, aunts, uncles, etc.—have been included only if they lacked other emotional or financial resources. This is the model of the *traditional family*. With cultural and economic changes, the traditional family evolved into what is defined as the *nuclear family*, composed exclusively of parents and children, other relatives being excluded from the immediate household.

The family is currently undergoing yet another change. We view this shift as being from the traditional, through the nuclear, and toward the *balanced family*.

Family insularity is becoming practically impossible. In our contemporary society *all* institutions are undergoing changes. They impinge more on one another, and they demand greater and greater commitment from those involved in them. Increasingly, we see our world divided into participants, observers, and the alienated. In our view, the balanced family must be numbered among the participants. We believe that such a stable family can infuse health and stability into the institutions with which its members interact, as well as deriving stimulation and a broadening perspective from them.

As we hope we've made clear, leadership roles in our institutions seldom come easily, or as a result of lucky breaks; they must be earned through a combination of talent, motivation, hard work, and an ability to anticipate and direct change. Similarly, a balanced family will not be achieved through a happy accident, but only through conscious striving and dynamic adaptation to the everychanging demands of our society. We have seen time and again that the quality of *deliberate effort* must be common to leadership

* Hendin, Herbert, in *The Age of Sensation*. Quoted by Robert J. Donovan in the *Los Angeles Times*, August 12, 1975.

and to successful family life. Not surprisingly, many people who are motivated to achieve leadership status are also motivated to create and sustain successful family relationships, and for many of the same reasons. Such achievement-oriented individuals perceive the need for stressing positives and for developing stable elements in a changing world. They also sense the possibilities for controlling and determining change to some significant extent.

New Definitions—New Obligations

In a balanced family each member is directed toward maintaining the family group and is also a contributing part of broader institutions. Each person is recognized within the family as an individual, with personal needs and the right to make personal decisions. The involvements of each individual in institutions outside the family are welcomed as sources of enrichment to the family group, and are respected as constructive contributions to society. These involvements are perceived as an important part of family life and are actively shared in the home environment. The family interrelates with, influences, and is influenced by many institutions.

Clearly, the balanced family we are describing is an evolving form not yet typical in this country, although the beginnings are very apparent. As examples, look at such outwardly directed family-related movements as housewives' consumer boycotts; the restructuring of the head of household role to be filled by either male or female partner or a combination of the two; parents' acceptance (however grudging) of kids' alternate lifestyles; intergenerational campaigns for new drug and abortion laws; expanding employment opportunities for married women; and cooperative day-care centers for working parents.

We believe that a balanced family, actively linked to other social institutions, stands a good chance of being healthy and productive in our present social climate. We must keep in mind that the balanced family, as we see it, is a dynamic, not yet fully realized, entity.

The balanced family can form the nucleus of a more balanced society, enriching the institutions with which its members interact.

It is imperative for leaders in all areas to become sensitive to the potential importance of the balanced family unit in the development of a strong and stable society. If the family is to survive as an institution for social good, leadership families *must* become forerunners of this evolutionary process, pioneering the new territory, and experiencing both the rewards and the hardships of being in the vanguard of social change. This responsibility to initiate positive change is a corollary of leadership.

We desperately need a new order of leadership to serve as role models and to begin moving us in a positive direction—toward integrity, credibility, and social responsibility. As a business leader, you will be a leader of change. You and other leaders will be compelled to be both more responsive and more responsible than your counterparts have been in the past. Society has changed: so must its leaders. In tomorrow's society the days of privilege without commitment, and the freedom to indulge in private indiscretions without impairment of public roles, will vanish. We'll talk about this further in a later chapter.

We'll return now to an important point that we touched on earlier. Leaders in the future must be prepared to help shape constructive change. They must also be prepared to assume responsibility for *resisting* change. We can no longer afford "progress at any price." Our leaders must develop a perspective that allows them to predict whether specific social changes have real merit— for the leader's own family, for the community, and for society at large. Increasingly, leaders of all institutions, in order to be socially effective, must have the inner strength and stability to stand up and resist changes that they believe are meaningless or negative. This is a difficult posture, and will certainly expose the individual leader to harsh criticism, but he or she must be prepared to accept attacks.

It is essential that each decision for or against change should be considered in terms of the maximum benefit to the greatest number of people. Leaders must recognize that in most situations instant decisions are not necessary or even desirable. Immediate value judgments can be counterproductive, and leaders must be strong enough to wait, gather necessary information, and *then* make commitments for or against action. Further, effective leadership demands that decisions be assessed and feedback considered. If a wrong decision has been made, it must be acknowledged and then rectified without fear of exposing the leader's human fallibility.

The kind of new leadership we feel *must* emerge will demand more than the dedication of the individual leader. Active participation of family members in outside institutions will be increasingly necessary, because the number and complexity of the institutions in contemporary society will require too great a commitment for one person to handle alone. Awareness of sharing the leadership role can help family members to cope with a direct challenge: to show that individual responsibility and commitment outside of self can intensify personal satisfaction.

Commitment of each family member to the goals and responsibilities of leadership is a beautiful ideal, but in our less than perfect world it is unlikely to happen in most families. It is inevitable that certain family members, especially children, will require special fence-building to protect them against the strains of their position. In other cases a spouse or one or more children may reject the demands of being a special family or may disagree with stated leadership goals. In such instances, if the family has an US relationship, open communication may resolve the conflict, or at least may lead to acknowledgment of an impasse. For example, parents committed to leadership goals may finally be forced to say to a child who is equally committed to an alternate lifestyle, "We don't agree with you, and we certainly don't approve of your values, but we love *you*. Whatever our conflicts, we're still a family." Other families, lacking this closeness and mutuality of respect and affection, may not survive intact when faced with such internal conflicts.

A balanced family that is built on an US relationship already has a protective framework to rely on. If one member is *not* ready or able to handle a social role outside the family, that individual is still loved, supported, and respected. One child of an executive family that followed the balanced family approach, while probably not calling it that, is now a wife and mother and trying to achieve a similar balance in her own new family. She says that the one thing she remembers from her childhood is never having to question who she *was*—her personhood was understood and accepted. And she claims that during her teens, even at the time when peer pressure was the most persuasive and confusing, she had enough security of self to make independent decisions. Feeling this security of self, she also felt comfortable in relating to people outside her family and peer group, and in participating in outside activities.

Now, let's look at the ways in which the members of a balanced leadership family interact with the larger society.

EXECUTIVE FUTURE CHALLENGES

We hope that you are interested in working to have a balanced family. If so, consider how you might handle these problems.

1. The company in which one of you is a rising executive has just moved one of its major divisions into a hostile community. The local citizens are antagonistic to this division because they fear environmental contamination. With a balanced family orientation how do you build "fences" for your family while you all adjust to your new community?

2. One child in your executive family has joined, and is actively participating in, a special interest group which is vocally attacking big business. The business leader in your family, and the corporation that leader represents, are among the targets under attack by your child's group. If you have a balanced family, how might you resolve this situation?

9

The Balanced Leadership Family in an Information Society

As we've suggested, you and other leadership families will have a responsibility to create a model for the new balanced family. You must be more attuned to social change than are families in more conventional circumstances. Members of your family will no longer be able to function by adhering to a system of guidelines or by following commandments laid down by a patriarchal head of household; they won't have the freedom just to proceed from crisis to crisis, grabbing at interim solutions. As participants in a new, balanced leadership family you must be motivators and trend setters; you must anticipate and constantly reassess and test linkages between individuals and the family unit, between the family and social institutions, and among various institutions with which individual family members interact!

Dynamics of the Leadership Family in Transition

If that sounds tough, it will be! That's why we keep hammering away at the essentials. Be an US, if you can. Have an A-Friend to bounce your anxieties and insecurities against, and to help you see how your own perceptions may be distorted. Have an Umbrella Theory that lets you accept other values for other people without challenging your own. With these tools and a lot of good luck, your leadership family may make it through the rough days ahead.

As a couple striving for a balanced leadership family, it is critically important for you to recognize—and to teach your children—that constant happiness is an unattainable goal. We see all around us the effects of the pleasure-first principle, especially in young people whose pursuit of instant gratification leads them from thrill to thrill, never satisfied with less, always needing more. Children from affluent leadership families must be carefully protected from this course—which means that you, as parents, must be fully aware of its risks.

The skills you develop and use in creating and sustaining such demanding relationships as an US will be put to the test in working with other families and social institutions. The social tools crucial for your leadership family will become increasingly important for all families in the emerging society. In fact, they will form the principal link extending the value systems of stable family units into the institutions of contemporary Western civilization—business, government, and educational institutions, in particular.

If all of this seems too theoretical, think about how to extend a balanced relationship to people and institutions outside your family. Say you begin on a simple level by sharing certain activities with other families. A sort of voluntary extended family can evolve. If you are avid campers or backpackers, you might include in your own family's activities the children of more sedentary parents. One of your own kids might have a scientific, musical, or literary bent that could be stimulated by a chance to take part in the pursuits of part-time "foster parents" with similar interests and abilities.

Such sharing of activities can enrich all the participants, and can allow each individual to develop fully his or her own special interests and talents. This kind of arrangement also can help to relieve parents of guilt for sometimes being unavailable to their children, or for being unable to excel at or enjoy every activity of interest to their kids.

Let us give an example of how this worked in our own family. While our children were growing up, they shared a phenomenon common to many executive families—an absent father. They understood and could often accept the reasons for their father's frequent absences from home, but still it was sometimes rough when *other* kids were having backyard barbecues, beach trips, and Indian Guide projects. Luckily, the father next door was engaged in another line of work and was almost always at home. He was available to play football and go to the beach and do all the good things our kids wanted to do. He was also the kind of guy who could warmly and happily include our brood with his, and could play surrogate father with delight.

Later we had a chance to reciprocate the kindness he had shown our family when one of his own children developed a definite interest in a scientific field with which the father was totally unfamiliar. We were able to take *that* child into our family and introduce him to ideas and experiences that he couldn't have had at home, and were able to encourage his educational and professional development in the field he chose. Happily, the children of both families were able to have the best of all possible worlds by enjoying the experiences and reinforcement two loving families could provide.

From such simple beginnings, your leadership family can move outward to share experience, abilities, and even your special knowledge of managing IT mechanisms. Sharing can occur within the framework of all the institutions in which various members participate. Of course as a business leader you will bring special insights and abilities to your professional role. The professional area is the first one in which you, as a potential leader, must excel and become recognized.

If one member of your couple does not participate in a career outside the home, but prefers to be more active in civic or cultural affairs or in child rearing, this person has an outstanding opportunity to introduce leadership skills and sophisticated IT techniques into such activities and to help create a positive environment in the community through participation in day-care centers, PTA, scouting, or other child-centered activities; through membership in politically oriented or social reform organizations; through civic beautification, music, or art organizations; or through charitable organizations.

Your children, taught by your example, can pass on to their peers what they have experienced, and can share with other young-sters the benefits derived from the special kind of listening they will learn as part of your US relationship: hearing, understanding, and then agreeing or disagreeing. It really isn't all that difficult to begin reaching outward!

If your leadership family is an US, individual family members will be better prepared to extend their roles outside the family because they'll be assured of their own special worth. And they will be in a better position to withstand the demands of leadership. The support and reassurance generated in the family relationship will be especially important as children become adolescents. At that time in their lives, young people are frantically searching for identity and a special individuality. For children reared as part of an US, this search can be far less painful because the individual identity has been recognized, nurtured, and respected almost from birth.

To encourage your own children in their quest for identity, you can consciously recognize and value the unique personality of each child. Strive deliberately to create an environment in which respect for every individual—within *and* outside the family—is basic. Children raised in such a climate are more likely to develop and retain a sense of self that can better withstand the traumas of adolescence, and can more readily tolerate the pressures of being part of a leadership family.

Leadership Roles: Creating an Environment

Whether you're facing struggle and sacrifice, or enjoying affluence, as parents in a leadership family you must consciously exert a special effort to create a framework for your family's existence. Within the special environment you create for your family and for friends, neighbors, and even corporate families, it is possible to control to a degree the influences of the outside world.

The capacity to create a personal environment is not peculiar to leaders: a young couple in love, new parents, kindergarten teachers, and camp counselors on rainy days are all examples of people who create self-contained environments in which personal attitudes and interpretations color and shape external realities. Nearly everybody can call to mind situations in which one individual helped to sustain an entire group by deliberately focusing attention on positive goals, humorous aspects of a crisis, or continuing effort in the face of disappointment.

Because of your special position relative to the world outside, members of your leadership family will have to work harder than most people to establish an environment for one another in which the emphasis is on stability, dedication to family goals, mutual affection, and gratification in individual and shared accomplishments. In your special environment, each individual should feel encouraged to do his or her best, and should be free to express opinions and beliefs, to develop talents and interests, and to air gripes. As the art of creating such a positive and reinforcing environment is developed within your immediate family, it can be extended into the corporate family, professional groups, schools, churches, and community and social organizations, with which family members interact.

Let's look at creating an environment in terms of the business leader. The way in which the chief executive officer (CEO) of a company conducts him or herself, and the attitudes that the CEO displays toward the people in the company, influence the kind of company that develops. As the parent figure in the special family that is the corporation, one CEO might stress informality and openness in the environment, seeking maximum communication and creativity from junior executives and nonmanagement people. He or she might carry over this personal style into social relationships within the corporation, choosing to entertain at home in a casual manner at barbecues and swimming parties, informal brunches, or family dinners. A more rigid chief executive would create a very different atmosphere on the job. In the social sphere his or her personality might be expressed by entertaining very formally or not at all.

Some executives strive to create a positive, comfortable environment for co-workers, while others seem deliberately to create a negative, threatening atmosphere. The president of one large bank created an environment that reflected his own paranoic personality. He was high-handed and dictatorial in dealings with employees, and enforced a rigid pecking order. He actively encouraged ruthless competition for promotion, and made employees acutely uncomfortable and insecure—from the tellers in the front office right up to the vice president who reported directly to him. The tension he created became so pervasive after a time that many people hired by the bank remained there only until they could find other employment. One young executive associated with the bank at present told us that although he is actively seeking another position, he feels he's gained something positive from his experience seeing first-hand how the personality of the president has affected the behavior of the entire staff. This young man is convinced that environment creation is a powerful tool, and hopes for a chance to create an atmosphere in his *own* corporation in which colleagues and subordinates will be challenged and motivated to succeed, seeking promotions for merit rather than getting ahead by back-stabbing.

In our own business experience, we've often seen how professional wives of executives can have a great part in creating an environment for the corporate family, as well as for their own families. Over the years we've enjoyed seeing the creativity some executive wives demonstrate when faced with sacrifices that would overwhelm less professional people. One friend, whose husband was an executive in a major oil company, found herself faced with a special problem when she and her children traveled with him on a tour of duty in a remote outpost in a developing Latin American country. Corporation families were all housed in an enclave miles from civilization, and our friend recognized immediately the kind of frustration that was developing among this little group of English-speaking families, totally isolated from their own country and also from the people of the country in which they were living.

She wanted to throw up her hands, but instead she got busy organizing a few communal activities, such as a day-care center to free young mothers from constant child-centered involvements. ("If nothing else," she claimed, "the day-care center gave each of us time to cry alone.'') Her enthusiasm stimulated others, and soon the women had started a book club, which both encouraged intellectual communication among adults and served to keep the stranded families in touch with the real world. Once the barriers of misery were broken down, the group launched other activities, and began to function as a real community. Instead of focusing on the many negatives in their situation, they really explored their unusual opportunity to shape their own society and create a tolerable environment for themselves.

While our friend's experience may seem a little extreme, there are constant opportunities for professional executive spouses to create environments for their own and corporate families. One woman whose husband was creating a management team made it her business to help new families moving into the corporate offices. Since getting the best people for the company meant moving in young executives from all over the country, it also meant considerable disruption of families—long and exhausting hours at work for the executives, and long and lonely hours for their spouses and kids, often in a bewildering new environment.

Even though neither her husband nor anyone else in the corporation asked her to do this, our friend made it part of *her* job to be on hand to greet newcomers. She would listen to their woes, help with house hunting, sit with their kids, clue them in to good shopping and other essentials, and generally make them feel as much a part of the corporate family life as she herself felt. In helping them to deflect their frustrations into channels that weren't destructive to their own families, she also inspired many of them to do a similar service for the next wave of newcomers. And the executive husbands, with relaxed and busy wives, found they had more time and energy to devote to their work—a fact that was appreciated and acknowledged by our friend's senior executive husband, who considered his wife an important asset to his career.

The women we've just described were both professional wives, and both happened to be warm, outgoing people who were at ease with people and interested in them. Either of them would be insulted if she were considered a pawn of the corporation, or if anyone believed that she was being exploited by her husband. Other professional wives who are less comfortable in group-oriented activities have just as much opportunity to create and extend positive environments. Consider some close friends of ours who moved to Washington, D.C., when the husband—a successful businessman—was appointed to an important government post. It was the first time the family had been separated: the wife and younger children went to Washington, but the older children remained behind to complete their education.

Shortly after the family's arrival in the capital, the husband became involved in the midst of a partisan conflict and was the target of considerable attention in the press. As is too often the case, he was attacked not only for his key role in the unpopular administration, but was also singled out for personal abuse. His wife had survived his long, hard struggle for business success, and had kept their children closely involved in a positive home environment and a common pride in their father's accomplishments. She was both appalled and angry that her children should now be subjected to near-slanderous attacks on their father, particularly at a time when they couldn't all sit down for a discussion of what was happening to him. Her response was to write a long open letter to the family, describing to the children the happiness she and her husband shared, and her continuing pride in his honesty and goodness. She outlined his many contributions to business, to government, and to his family, and she retraced for her kids the circumstances of the family's past life together and the present political situation that was being experienced now by only part of them. By presenting her perspective, and relating it to what they knew of their father from their own experience, she was able to share with her children an emotional environment in which they could continue to be proud and supportive of their father, irrespective of the slurs being made against him.

A final example suggests the ingenuity sometimes demanded in creating a positive personal environment for an executive family. The husband, a design engineering whiz kid, met a major career challenge in the early days of computers. Almost at the completion date for a new computer memory design—a crucial contract for a young and growing company—he discovered that there was a serious error in his model. To pull the project out of the fire within the contract time limits, he was forced to work virtually around the clock for several weeks, catching naps on a cot in his office, and then getting back to work. While he stayed permanently on duty, he required support from several technicians and staff people, all of whom had to remain in the plant almost constantly during the critical period.

The engineer had a wife and several small children, and like his colleagues was forced to be separated from his family for the duration of the emergency. His wife, aware of the importance of the project and the pressure he was under, did her part to lend support and to help relieve the tension at the plant. At the same time she helped to maintain the close ties between her children and their dad. Every few days she would arrive at the plant, bearing clean clothes for her husband, and a picnic dinner for him and his co-workers, and she'd bring along all the kids. They had a chance to talk to their father and tell him about *their* activities, and they also were able to learn first-hand about what he was doing. Rather than feeling rejected because of his absence, their mother helped them to feel proud and excited that their daddy was such an important man with such a hard job.

In all of these examples the executive wives, who had chosen careers as homemakers, were truly professional. And all of them felt both challenged and fulfilled by the special demands presented by their husband's careers. One of our pet peeves is the recent spate of articles and books about the tragedy of the company-wife syndrome. One of our friends summed it up beautifully. She'd just read the latest book about unhappy, unfulfilled, alcoholic, sex-crazed victims of corporate transfers and company attitudes toward wives, and she said "How come we've never *met* any of these women? I feel as if I've really missed something. I would have been a miserable neurotic if I'd known I was supposed to—but I've just been too busy!" She couldn't deny, of course, that many wives of executives (and milk men, and housepainters) *are* miserable. She just didn't agree that it was all part of the corporate-wife package. And as a matter of fact, she was too busy to meet those women who couldn't cope. Sometimes it seems as if the only people who *do* have time to listen to such women are some of the journalists who write about them. And those journalists rarely, if ever, see the other side of the coin: those who are living happy, productive, and *private* lives in a very positive environment which they have created!

As we have suggested in this chapter, getting to be a balanced family will require conscious and continuing effort from all members of your family. The transition within your family will occur in the same time frame with accelerated external changes, which may also produce new strains on your relationship.

EXECUTIVE FUTURE CHALLENGES

In the preceding chapter we've talked about some of the actual processes involved in becoming the kind of balanced, leadership family that can control its inner environment and interact with the outer one. Think in those terms as you consider the following situations, and how you would meet them.

1. You (wife) are married to a fast-rising executive in a large corporation. You are also a young women who is sensitive to your own personhood. You (husband) are trying to develop a good workable management team and you ask for your wife's support in helping the other wives to understand the demands made on their husbands. You (wife) are unsure of your reactions: after all, this isn't *your* job. And are the other wives going to think you're interfering, or even pandering for the company?

2. You're a new manager in an isolated community. There are about thirty families living in this geographic nowhere, and all of them are involved with your operation. Many of the families are actively unhappy, and are developing serious problems that are threatening to destroy your operation. Key personnel are on the verge of leaving. How can you help alleviate the frustration they are feeling?

10

Leadership Families in a Crunch

From what we've already said about the roles and responsibilities of the leadership family, you may think such a family is *always* in a crunch! There are, however, certain very ordinary circumstances (ordinary, at least, in nonleadership families) that can throw a leadership family into a tailspin if they have not been discussed and planned for ahead of time.

A problem can occur if the leader's changing role in family life has not been anticipated. Resentments can arise when a career homemaker in a leadership family suddenly is made to feel unfulfilled in her role. And the almost inevitable clash of two demanding careers in the ever-more-common two-career family can create an enormous problem, as can the birth of a child in such a family.

The tools we have described—a systems approach to planning, an US, effective use of IT, A-Friends, the Umbrella Theory, and management of the time resource, can all be applied to these problems. But it is essential for the leadership couple to determine early whether a commonality of goals is possible for them, because the circumstances of a leadership career can produce terrible strains on the family that might become unbearable without the active commitment of both marriage partners.

Status Changes in the Family

Generally speaking, in what we have described as typical or conventional business leadership families—those with one aspiring executive member—the end goal of a young, upwardly mobile couple
is closely tied to the prospective leader's career. The family's daily
life is influenced by, and to a great extent focused on, the executive's efforts to reach and sustain a top-level management position.
The ultimate aim is probably the position of Chief Executive Officer, with alternate acceptable levels below that position. (Comparable goals for political leaders might be the presidency, election
to the Senate, or a governorship.) For executive families headed
up the corporate ladder, the money constraint is typically over-
come rather early. The next most pressing problem is probably
reaching agreement about the degree to which the executive's ambition dominates the family's life.

In emerging from a long training period into the real world of
business, the young executive is filled with tremendous drives toward instant achievement. Often he or she not only works hard,
but works constantly, and the creativity and enthusiasm that characterize the executive's personality are narrowly focused on attain-
ment of immediate goals. Spouse and children must be prepared to
accept absences and the redirection of attention and energy without feeling rejected and victimized. They must not feel abandoned,
merely postponed! A habit of open, honest communication is the
surest means of surviving the ships-passing-in-the-night syndrome.

If the spouse is willing to accept the executive's goal orientation, and actively support it, the aspiring CEO stands a much better
chance of reaching those goals. We feel especially close to couples
facing the demands of an executive life, which requires enormous
contributions from every family member. Supporting the ego and
ambition of a rising executive requires much grace, humor, and
endurance!

Creativity: It's in the Eyes of the Beholder

When the rising executive is the husband, and when the wife has
chosen a career in the home, special problems can arise. Faced

with her husband's growing success and recognition, a creative homemaker can sometimes be made to feel totally worthless because her excellent services do not have an established monetary value. Millions of homemakers have been sold a bill of goods about the busy, creative days spent by those who go out to be part of the work force. In fact, virtually every salaried position, from shoe salesperson to company president, is about 80 percent sheer, boring drudgery, with a maximum of 20 percent creative or exciting achievement.

now they tell us!

On balance, we've discovered, the woman who chooses a career in the home may spend more creative and rewarding time in the course of a single day than does her professional husband in his entire week! A wife may be more sympathetic with her husband when he comes home frustrated and unhappy if she realizes that his exciting day may not be all that it is cracked up to be. No matter how important his title, or how vital his role in the organization, chances are that only parts of some days are truly stimulating.

Years ago, as a still-new executive couple, we assessed typical days in our respective careers: Ronya's dull days at home with small children, compared with George's dramatic life as a corporate executive. The results were enlightening! George had been spending a great deal of time in Washington, trying to sell a major military program for his company. Although he was eventually successful, he had still spent most of each day for six months sitting in outer offices, waiting for various government representatives to give him an hour or less of their time: one hour of creative time against six or seven hours of tedium and frustration. The boring routines of homemaking suddenly seemed less oppressive!

Many executives are, as George was during those months, very well read in *Sports Illustrated, National Geographic,* and other waiting-room fare. When an executive husband conveys this aspect of his professional life to his homemaker wife, she can recognize that her own day is not altogether different. She can appreciate that while the dull tasks included in a typical day—washing diapers, grocery shopping, picking up toys—may well take up 70 to 80 percent of her time, she may also have a good 20 or 30 percent free in which to read a book, play tennis, do needlepoint, or perform volunteer or community work that gives her much pride and satisfaction. The important point is for both husbands and wives to understand and appreciate the gray areas of one another's days.

Such understanding is one technique for reinforcing a young woman who chooses a career as a homemaker. We hope that through systems thinking, a working US, A-Friends who can appreciate them, and an Umbrella Theory that helps them experience, without absorbing, new attitudes, such young women can avoid some of the emotional pitfalls that have been experienced by many of their older counterparts. A great many older career homemakers have been caught in a new ballgame where they don't understand the rules.

The current glorification of women working outside the home has forced many mature women, even among the affluent leadership group, to feel they must seek outside employment to validate their worth as people. Today 50 to 60 percent of adult women work outside the home and earn salaries. Current thinking suggests that a person is of value only if his or her work is financially compensated. This cast of mind, coupled with downgrading of the homemaker's role, has thrown many women into an emotional spin.

The feeling of worthlessness experienced by such women in our society represents a problem that must be dealt with soon. These women are painful living examples of how our society has been caught up in attitudinal shifts that have made innocent victims of a whole generation of female citizens.

The Two-Career Family

Once exceptional, the two-career family is growing in importance in our contemporary society. Time and labor-saving devices in the home, easy-care clothing, and—in many cities—excellent day-care facilities have freed women to realize their potential in career areas other than homemaking. Among business and other leadership families, where high mobility is common, the demands of two professional careers (as distinct from one career and one interchangeable job) are potentially disruptive to the balanced family.

As we've mentioned earlier, we've known extraordinary couples who could keep families intact while successfully pursuing two careers in two widely separated locations, and this is—for some leadership families—a workable alternative. Like other options available to couples caught in the two-career crunch, this one is best considered coolly, well before the crunch occurs.

In planning the future of a two-career family, several variables should always be considered. Does either of the two careers involve a high degree of mobility? Do both? Is the more stationary of the two careers likely to offer plenty of opportunities in the geographic areas where the other career is likely to lead? (As an extreme example, if one career is with a world wide oil company, the spouse with the second career may stand a poor chance of finding satisfactory employment at many of the remote temporary posts to which the oil company will dispatch its executives.) Is one career dependent on permanence—such as building up a private medical, legal, or accounting practice?

The potential for career conflict need not represent an insurmountable problem. And the ideal time for a confrontation on the subject is before job offers are considered. At the very least this discussion should occur in early career stages, before the first major development in one partner's career poses a threat to the other.

In two-career marriages, even more than in the conventional single-career family, it is imperative to apply systems techniques in formulating and reassessing multiple long-term goals. One step in such a projection, once the likelihood of career conflict is acknowledged, is to establish which of the partners has the primary career: which career will determine the couple's course with respect to accepting job offers, promotions, or transfers over time.

Such an analysis becomes more difficult where one of the partners does not have a readily marketable skill and may have to face the search for an entirely new career or business. Using the systems approach, the situation can be forecast early, and options can be formulated that may help to minimize the trauma and expedite a solution before the problem becomes overwhelming. Advance planning and anticipation of the circumstances of career change can make the transition easier by shortening the time interval between positions. The briefer the period in limbo, the lesser the risk of insecurity for the partner caught in the change.

One couple, graduates of our executive futures seminar, began by listing all possible career alternatives involved in the development of their two careers. Gradually they eliminated those that were clearly impossible, those they considered intolerable, and those that were most objectionable. What they had left ranged from optimal to at least workable within their framework of objectives and constraints. Thus, they were able to determine realistically which career should take priority at this early stage.

Typically, at the present time, it is usually the husband's career that takes precedence. Even now that may change when the wife in the couple is the more ambitious, when she specializes in a field that promises greater achievement, or when the husband's career is the more easily transferable from one location or industry to another. Whichever partner's career is considered primary by the couple, in a systems approach to goal-setting, this is not a permanent decision. As the family's circumstances change and one or the other partner moves up the leadership ladder, different priorities can be assigned.

We've recently had the pleasure of watching the success of a systems approach to planning a two-career family. Both members of the young couple were accounting specialists. He was a CPA, working with one of the Big Eight companies, while she was completing her doctorate with an eye toward teaching at a particular university. The couple agreed before he took his first job that he would progress with the company he had chosen until such time as she earned her Ph.D. At that point he would transfer his highly marketable skills to the city of her choice. His talents were noticed, and he was quickly promoted. In fact, he was at the point of being made a partner of his very prestigious firm when she was awarded her doctorate. But he didn't renege on their agreement; an offer was forthcoming from the university she had sought, and the couple accepted it without hesitation. The husband quickly found work with an independent accounting firm in the new city, and is once again working his way through the ranks to a partnership.

In another two-career family, it is the man's career that is guiding our young friends' early years out of school. The inflexible demands of the young husband's career restricted him to a particular location, while the wife's most attractive job offers came from other cities hundreds of miles from that site. The couple chose to live together on a regular basis rather than commute on weekends, and so the wife voluntarily accepted the least appealing of her opportunities in order to work in the same metropolitan area with her husband. Even though they had agreed upon this course of action previously, she admits she can't help feeling great resentment over her diminished role. Being able to vocalize her anger in several forthright griping sessions with a woman A-Friend has helped her to handle it without blaming her husband.

As we mentioned in chapter 3, two dynamic young professionals in a two-career marriage may suddenly find their relationship under a great strain if one of them experiences a strong nesting urge while the other is still committed to a goal of achieving material comforts. Usually, this happens as the wife nears thirty, often about the time the couple has begun to achieve leadership and financial objectives. On the other hand, when open communication between the couple establishes a common desire for children, systems planning can help them to enjoy the rewards of both their leadership career and of parenting.

A severe time constraint is one significant by-product of two-career marriages. With both members of a couple working long hours outside the home, and both involved in business-related social and professional obligations after hours, there simply isn't adequate time to accomplish everything. It is especially important for such couples to budget their time, and to decide together what has to give. Some couples may choose to give up house-cleaning duties, evenings at the movies, or nonbusiness travel. Others may choose to remain childless, devoting to other activities the time that children would demand. Whichever way the individual couple establishes priorities, the important thing is for them to discuss and agree on which are essential and which are dispensable time commitments from each of them.

Some business and other institutions, realizing the significance of time constraints in two-career families, are making adjustments to accommodate employees. An example is "flexi-time," in which the employee is permitted to adjust his or her schedule to coincide with other demands. Another approach that is being explored, especially in academic institutions, is for each partner to work half time, sharing home and family responsibilities during the other half day. As increasing numbers of two-career families seek solutions to the problem of time limitation, we'll see many innovative arrangements for balancing career and family.

Aside from its impact on the life of leadership families, the two-career marriage in going to have substantial influence over the next decade on the lives of corporations, government agencies, and other institutions. Corporations will no longer be able to disregard the spouse's commitments when transferring a business executive. Already some industrial leaders have taken the initiative in helping to find comparable employment for a marriage partner when they move a promising young star. Other signs are more generous and flexible maternity leaves for female executives, company-sponsored day-care centers, and even paternity leaves for fathers who wish to share in child care.

Keeping It Together

The life of an executive or other leader isn't an easy one. A person committed to leadership in business and management often must move from one crisis to another, with little breathing time. For the few individuals strong enough, dedicated enough, and talented enough to make it to the top, the active encouragement and support of an understanding and committed family can be an essential ingredient in success. Every leadership family goes through different stages of self-awareness and shifting relationships within the group and with the outside world. As the pressures and problems of executive life become reality, family communication should be enlarged to include the new life experiences of all members. At a very early stage a mechanism should be developed for reaching decisions that have significance both to the family and to the further development of the leader's career.

To give the leader the kind of support and reinforcement possible in a balanced family, and to give the family the rewards of an exciting and worthwhile life, it is important for every leadership family to plot an individual life chart, such as the one shown on page 25. As they plan and readjust to the demands of their hectic life, family members should be aware of the forty-year life span that a leadership family faces together. This kind of awareness in a couple in their twenties can help them to arrive, forty years later, at a relationship that is still growing and enriching.

Just recently, there seems to have been an epidemic of divorces in a group of our friends who had been married between twenty-five and thirty-five years. The divorces seemed to coincide with the departure of children from the home. This pattern seems increasingly common, particularly among the affluent who do not have to stay together for financial reasons. A series of such divorces poses a kind of subtle threat to those of us whose marriages remain intact.

Shortly after we'd been through—and were still disturbed by —several of these dissolved marriages, we attended a meeting of the board of directors of a particular company. Once a year this board meets and invites the spouses of both board members and corporate officers to attend. Most of the board members were in the forty to sixty-five age range, and they were men and women who were top achievers in other companies, in banks, and in several professions. We were struck by the relationships between the spouses at this gathering. Most of the couples had been married twenty-five years or more, their children had left the nest, and they were entering a new phase of life as "just a couple" again. What moved both of us was the love, affection, and eagerness to be together that these couples displayed.

As we grew to know them better, we realized that through the years each spouse had brought something very special to the relationship, so that instead of diluting the feelings within the marriage, they had helped to intensify them. Each partner seemed to have grown as an exciting person individually as well as growing within the marriage. Each had achieved special value and dignity as a person, and this was both recognized and sought by the other partner. Interestingly, about half the women in these couples had outside careers, and half were homemakers. Those who *were* homemakers were what we like to call professional wives. Their husbands not only recognized the importance of this role, but through the years had reinforced their wives by constantly valuing them as people.

We believe that such successful executive marriages as these are never written or talked about because they are so quiet and personal. We suggest that there are *many* of these marriages, and that they can be achieved if young people consciously start at the beginning of their marriage with a goal of celebrating their twenty-fifth wedding anniversary as an exciting cooperative event. Leadership families should consciously become models for this kind of relationship. The goal of a successful, fulfilling marriage—an US relationship—should be concurrent with career fulfillment goals for both spouses.

But, keeping your goal for your twenty-fifth anniversary in mind, let's turn to a subject of more immediate practicality. In the next chapters we'll explore how the aspiring business leader becomes a real professional—starting with his or her first executive position.

EXECUTIVE FUTURE CHALLENGES

There are many crises that you will face in moving toward your end goal. Some of these crises will be immediate if you are starting out together as a two-career family.

1. You are a two-career family. Both of you are young, ambitious, and highly motivated to achieve in your separate careers. You have been working at being an US. Gradually it's becoming apparent that you (husband), although ambitious, are not an outstanding performer in your chosen field. In the meantime, you (wife) are gaining considerable recognition in your area. You (husband) are supportive, and proud of these achievements, but occasional feelings of jealousy are creeping in, and causing friction. You (wife) feel hurt and put down, but you don't want to sacrifice either your career or your growing US relationship. How would the two of you solve this conflict?

2. You are a young two-career family. You (husband) have just been promoted to a job that requires a great deal of managerial

talent. You are under enormous pressure, and the strain is increasingly difficult. You require a great deal of sympathetic attention at home at this time. You (wife) are completing your doctoral dissertation, and the deadline for submission is rapidly approaching. You, too, need a lot of support and reinforcement at home. Which of you will be the more giving partner at this crucial point in your growing US relationship?

11

Professionalization of a Leader: Getting Started

Please take a minute to think about what this chapter means. You, as an aspiring leadership couple, are in the unique position of *planning* your future as leaders. Because you have consciously decided to follow this career path, you have the advantage of tools that will help you cope with the life crises you will assuredly face—starting with your first step up the leadership ladder.

In approaching earlier chapters, we have assumed a certain perspective: that of the leader on the move—the executive on the way up, the aspiring senator, the college president-to-be. Now we want to step back and take a preliminary look at this emerging leader. In the case of the business executive, for example, how does he or she get the first job? And keep it? And become established in the corporate hierarchy as an upwardly mobile entity? And, having accomplished these essential first steps, how does the leader stay on target, professionally and ethically? How does he or she retain a sense of perspective in the face of growing professional and public admiration and adulation? Through all of these processes, what part do spouse and family play at each stage of the leader's professionalization? Before proceeding, we should define the term professionalization as we apply it to the leader (and to the

111

leader's spouse). In our sense, professionalization is a combination of education plus experience on the job.

As a recent business school graduate, your first job will probably be in middle management. The leadership role is already significant at this level, and you will have ample opportunity to hone leadership skills for the long-range goal of a top management post. For a corporation to perform effectively today, leadership must be diffused through many levels of the organization, and not just filtered down from the top. You will have a distinct advantage as a new executive if you recognize, and are prepared to assume, the leadership function starting with your first position.

Now let's look at *you*, the prospective leader, and what's in store for you. But first things first! In order to become a top executive, or a leader in another area, it's necessary first to have a job! This is the time when potential business leaders, and their spouses, must start to do their stuff.

Preparing for the first job after school can be an agonizing experience. We've seen candidates make terrible errors by being over-confident and under-prepared in seeking a particular position. An US relationship can be especially important in avoiding this trap, and in helping the candidate to be effective as an interviewee. Here are a few how-to suggestions that we've seen work. If you're about to start interviewing for a first job, they will probably help you too.

Narrowing the Field

Before the first interview, you and your spouse should decide on some fundamental matters. First, where do you want to live? Would your spouse's career development be adversely affected if your position required relocating? Would frequent moves be a hardship? You should ask yourself where you want to be and what you want to be doing in five, ten, or fifteen years. You should consider how the initial job will fit into these plans.

You must also decide, within the framework of your intended career specialization as a business graduate, your immediate and long-range salary requirements, and the fringe benefits essential to your family's survival. You must consider any personal absolutes that prevail. For example, if one or the other of you is violently opposed to taking financial risks, or to such contingencies as living abroad, or being separated frequently, such strong feelings should be brought to the surface *immediately* to avoid later unhappiness and recriminations. The universe of potential employers should be structured accordingly.

The next step is for you as a would-be employee to compile a list of those companies in the relevant specialty area whose locations and expectations conform to your absolutes as a couple, and whose style, business ethic, and corporate structure are compatible with your own interests, personal ethic, and career objectives. As a candidate, you should consider whether a position with the company would stimulate the learning process and offer leadership potential in the chosen field. Then you must do some homework, concentrating on getting to *know* the company chosen for an interview.

One place to start is the library of a large brokerage firm or a university business school library. You should examine annual reports, and if possible a Standard & Poor report on the company. If the interviewing company is on the New York Stock Exchange, a good information source is Value-Line. You should analyze and *understand* the company's financial position, product line, and any other pertinent information that would show the interviewer what an active interest you have in the company.

Once as familiar as possible with the company's organization, operation, financial picture, growth pattern, prospects, and weaknesses, you should attempt to find the key to serving the company's interests through creative application of your own unique talents! This is not a small undertaking. In today's job market it's not simply a question of being prepared to fill a given position. What is demanded is that you become sufficiently self-aware and self-analytical to determine your true strengths and potential value to the organization, and also those weaknesses that might be a handicap. You should be *so* familiar with the company's needs and objectives that you can intermesh your personal qualifications with

the company interests. You should be able to create a job that
hasn't even been defined by the company. In short, you should be
prepared to sell yourself to the company.

We suggest that this crucial and difficult time is one occasion
when the observations and insights of a loving and supportive
spouse can be most valuable. Who is better prepared to reinforce
your self-awareness, to point out honestly, and without judgmental
overtones, your unperceived weaknesses, and to highlight your
special strengths, gifts, and abilities? If you are part of an US
relationship, you already have an advantage!

With all the homework done, it's time to make an initial contact with the company, either through a personal introduction, a
university recruitment program, or an introductory letter directed
to a specific, responsible corporate executive. Whichever approach you take, this initial contact is important: it must be carefully designed to inspire the company's interest, and to prompt an
employment interview.

The time of arranging your first job interview may be your
initial opportunity to use yet another leadership tool that you have
no doubt been developing since you started graduate school, although you may not have recognized it. We call this tool a "people
net," and it is something you should consciously cultivate and use,
despite the somewhat negative connotations attached to the simi-
lar-sounding "ole boy network." A people net is a network of
friends and acquaintances whose different specialties complement
your own. As you establish your first career position, you may
already be able to call on someone from your existing people net
to arrange an introduction into his or her company or to recom-
mend you to a company with which you want to interview.

As you begin moving upward in your career, you'll constantly
add to your people net. And when business or other leadership
problems require particular insights or talents outside the scope of
your organization, you'll often be able to draw on a perfect expert
from your people net. This is a reciprocal relationship: as your own
expertise grows, your talents will be called on as part of someone
else's people net. Alumni and professional organizations in various
disciplines should play an important role in building your people
net. They cannot only help you to keep current, but can also pro-

vide an opportunity to assess yourself and your personal growth in comparison with your peers.

The key to any thriving organization is the key people who make it grow, and the people nets on which they draw. As an executive, you'll be only as good as the people you can bring in from the outside to solve specific problems. The people net is one excellent reason why, when leaving any job or professional relationship, you should be extremely careful to end on a cordial note. No matter how difficult the circumstances of the parting, it's worth every effort to keep it pleasant. One day your situation may require renewed contact with former associates, and they'd better be a willing part of your people net!

Dry-Running

We've watched and counseled many a job applicant over the years, and we have consistently found that the best approach to successful interviewing is to go through one or more rehearsals, or "dry-run" interviews. It is during this phase of the job hunt that your spouse, an A-Friend, and perhaps a generous instructor can be of immeasurable help to you by performing the unpleasant task of conducting such dry-run interviews.

The dry-run interviewer puts her- or himself in the position of the corporate interviewer and attempts to anticipate the probing questions that the interviewer will ask you as a candidate. The dry runner should show little mercy in grilling you, exposing and attacking weak positions or statements, demanding firm and directly responsive answers, and company-directed benefits of the proposed working association. A well conducted dry-run interview, or a series of them, should anticipate about 90 percent of the questions that will be asked in the actual interview, and should prepare you emotionally for thinking quickly and responsively under pressure.

Some of the important questions you as a candidate should be prepared to answer are: Why am I interested in this business? Why am I interviewing for a job in this field? What rewards and satisfactions can I expect if I actually get a job offer from this company? What have I found out about the company that will demonstrate my interest? What can I bring to the company in the way of abilities and character traits? Why should the company hire me? What can I contribute? What am I looking for in this firm? What are my main reasons for wanting to join this particular company? How will I benefit from working for this company? Does the job I'm seeking fit my long-range goals?

The dry-run interviewer should formulate questions designed to bring out this information, and should analyze and criticize your answers in terms of the company's interests. This job is a vital one, and will be almost as exhausting for the dry-runner as it will be for you. We know this from experience.

The effort, however, is well worthwhile when the candidate is successful, as was one young man about whom we were especially concerned. He had worked for several years as an apprentice cameraman in the highly competitive television film industry when he was given an opportunity to compete for a much-coveted position in that industry.

The first hurdle was an examination designed to test professional aptitude, knowledge, and native talent. Fifteen hundred applicants took the exam, and the seventy who passed with highest scores were invited for personal interviews. Our young friend was one of the seventy, from whom ten would be selected to fill the positions available. He was frankly panicked. He had no qualms at all about his abilities to handle the job, and had demonstrated his grasp in the written exam. He was, however, terrified of the interview, recognizing his tendency to choke when he was forced to talk about himself. The evening before the interview his wife and his other A-Friend teamed up to dry-run him. They meticulously covered the ground they expected the real interviewer to cover, and told him frankly when his answers were less than inspiring. By the time *they* finished with him, the actual interview held few terrors! He was relaxed and confident, and it showed. As one of the lucky ten to win the prized position, he is convinced that for him the difference between succeeding and wiping out was the dry-run interview.

Moving in the Right Direction:
Up the Corporate Ladder

Once you are fortunate enough to connect with the right first job, the next step is to *keep it,* and to begin moving upward in the corporate structure by actually performing the kind of creative work promised in the interview! One element in keeping the job is constant assessment of how well you are doing it. This involves sensitivity to feedback from colleagues, some of it expressed, but much of it merely implied. This means you must be adept at reading signals and reacting to them, and also at filtering the unimportant noise (petty sniping or, alternatively, meaningless flattery) from the information (legitimate criticism or genuine compliments).

Clearly, doing a good job and learning to assess and react to feedback will require an enormous expenditure of time and energy on your part as a junior executive, and, as we have discussed previously, tremendous understanding, patience, and support from your spouse and family. This is the time when your executive spouse can help you retain your perspective, to interpret correctly feedback concerning your performance, to value your staff and other support personnel, and to avoid assiduously the "Lt. Shiny Newbars" syndrome. This is a good opportunity for your mate to apply the principles of constructive criticism.

One important rule concerning criticism (positive or negative) relates to timing. Compliments should be shared. Helpful, but negative, criticism should be conveyed privately. The same comments conveyed publicly, in front of children, relatives, or friends, *could* be totally destructive, and certainly wouldn't be constructive to the recipient. We believe criticism should be saved for the special time most couples set aside for themselves, either consciously or unconsciously. Then they are most free to discuss problems, frustrations, or triumphs. For us, it's always been bedtime, when the telephone has finally stopped ringing, the house is quiet, and for once we have total privacy. Then we feel particularly close to each other, and we can exchange criticism freely, knowing very well it will be private.

The Professional Wife: A Fellow Traveler

Returning to our example of the male executive and his professional wife (and make no mistake, the wife of an executive, or other top leader, must become professional at *that* job, whatever career she may pursue outside the home), this difficult time in the executive's career will make many demands on her. Not only will she be active in her own role, and in supporting him in his career advancement, but she will also be extremely busy building fences to protect the two of them and their children against outside critics of her husband's ambition, career involvement, and his long hours away from the family. And this is the time when she will begin to expand her role as the balanced family's link to community institutions, and the family's buffer against and an interpreter of IT inputs. In other words, the first years of the new executive's corporate life make tremendous demands on *both* partners!

Obviously, there are two ways the wife can react to the tensions and trials of this period. She can approach the many demands and inconveniences as a challenge, and consider meeting them as part of *her* professional obligation, or she can become a constant complainer, overwhelmed by the negative aspects of her position. If she chooses the latter course she will, of course, convey her own negativism to the couple's children, and to any outsiders with whom she communicates.

One friend of ours was a true professional wife who faced with equanimity her family's impending move to Little Rock, despite the fact that both she and her children were well established socially in their community and had achieved considerable prominence in civic affairs. When her husband was offered a substantial promotion that involved what could have been a wrenching move, she declined to bemoan her fate, but instead paid a visit to Little Rock, to explore what *that* community had to offer in the way of her own and the children's special interests. She worked with the chamber of commerce to discover the city's resources, and mapped out a tour for each family member, concentrating on the special activities of each one. By the time she returned from reconnoitering the new city, she was prepared to be enthusiastic herself, and to convey her enthusiasm to her family. The transition was made smoothly, owing largely to her attitude, and her recognition that *her* reactions would be reflected in those of the children.

The executive husband lucky enough to have attracted the interest and loyalty of such a wife should acknowledge her professionalism and appreciate the extent to which it enhances both his personal life and his career. Anyone foolish enough to take for granted such a gifted partner is risking both resentment and a breakdown of a strong relationship. To be an accomplished wife and mother under the exacting circumstances of a leadership situation requires as much creative ability and talent as does any other skilled profession.

When the wife is the executive, and the husband the partner who must adjust, equal enthusiasm and commitment is required. The role of professional husband is a newer one, less perfectly understood either by society or by those who find themselves occupying the role. It will be interesting to observe the ways in which our society will change to prepare boys to become men who will perform comfortably in this emerging social position.

The difficulty of this particular situation in our present society was brought home to us by a young couple, each with a career, who made an atypical decision. After the birth of their first child, their lifestyle was relatively unchanged. They still pursued their separate careers, and they were delighted with the day-care provisions they could make for their baby. In fact, it was all so perfect that they went ahead and had a second child, expecting the pattern to continue. Unfortunately, the perfect day-care arrangement was inadequate for a second child. Discussing the problem as mature adults, they decided that of the two of them, the wife/mother was the more ambitious and career oriented, and the husband/father more inclined to be the career homemaker. They resolved their difficulty by having her continue to work, and him stay at home, which for them proved to be a workable solution. Their families, however, were distressed and uncomfortable with the couple's role assignment and their unconventional adaptation to a career conflict.

In applying systems techniques to a leadership family, in striving to become a whole ME and part of a successful US, the key is to remain dynamic, always attuned to growth and change in each individual and in the relationship. So it is in the leadership career —a constant and conscious process of maturing.

EXECUTIVE FUTURE CHALLENGES

Now that you are aware of the pitfalls that may lay ahead in the world of business, be prepared to view your own situation in the light of becoming a professional leader.

1. You are about to graduate with an MBA, and you are starting to interview for a position. You've finished your first interview, and are feeling depressed. You haven't heard from the company, but you already know you've blown the interview. What do you do to ensure this won't happen next time?

2. You have just completed a series of very successful job interviews. This has taken three months while you have been finishing your professional report in graduate school. From your many interviews you have received five separate job offers from five different companies. How do you go about deciding which is the right job for you?

12

Professionalization of a Leader: Maturing on the Job

understatement
Ha! Ha!!

Most effective leaders aren't loved all the time. In fact, the ability to make hard decisions and to act for the greatest benefit of the corporation will make the leader unpopular with at least some employees. As we've seen in our own career, some of the most successful and creative top executives are feared and hated—but also mainly respected—by their employees. A leader should expect to be lonely and alienated far oftener than are people with less exalted aspirations.

You, as a prospective leader, should apply these principles in your own career. You can never let desire to be liked interfere with doing your job. Yet most of us do find it easier to work with people we like, and who like us. To be a successful leader, you must be prepared to take risks, and to recognize that the buck stops with you. You must constantly guard against letting your need for personal popularity undermine your objectivity in decision making. Within every organization there will be people eager to take potshots and to find flaws in your leadership. Critics will point out significant and insignificant omissions in your decisions and may spur others to dissatisfaction. As a leader, you must be prepared to survive in this environment. You must be secure in your own leadership qualities—strength of character, fairness, tough mind-edness, openness to ideas, and decisiveness—and you must set your guidelines accordingly.

When any key decision has to be made in a company, there will be groups that like the decision, and groups that don't. As a business executive you will have to trust yourself to evaluate the impact of your decision, and to assess the reponse to it—using your own ability to separate noise from information, often en-hanced by the reinforcement offered by your spouse and other A-Friends. You must develop the ability to consider your decisions not just in the narrow perspective of the good of the corporation, but in the much broader context of the good of the corporation in relation to the community and the nation. As you move up the corporate ladder, you must decide what combination of nice guy and stern taskmaster works best for you. You must learn from experience when to be tough-minded. You must provide a stable environment within your company so each member can make a meaningful contribution.

Opening Communication: The Answer Is Blowing in the Wind

In learning the job and becoming increasingly important to the company, you must learn to listen and to evaluate the inputs from all levels of the company—both those from executives who are your superiors in the organization, and those from junior execu-tives and operational employees. Naturally, this involves exercis-ing your own information filter when you listen to *any* input, but you must never reject out of hand information on what is happen-ing, or how the company's inner workings are viewed. Concom-mitant with listening to everyone is respecting each individual within the company for his or her special contribution and impor-tance. The overall functioning of the corporation is dependent on the functioning of each person, regardless of position or responsi-bility.

When you are discussing problems with, or listening to com-plaints from, any subordinate, it's important for you to understand that subordinate's function. If, for example, you are dealing with a production department foreman, you should know that department's operations. You should also know which operations precede, and which follow, the work of that department. Such understanding will enable you to assess what the foreman says to you, and to be aware of any preconceived notions being projected. This can help you focus correctly on the actual origin of the problem. Listening to and respecting the people who work with you is one way to establish yourself with them as a real person. Don't ever be afraid to roll up your sleeves and see your company from the workers' point of view. This can bring unforeseen benefits when you are let in on valuable insights missed by an aloof manager. If employees feel free to call your attention to mistakes at an early stage, this can give you an opportunity to acknowledge errors openly, and to correct them, without fear of betraying your fallibility and destroying your image.

What can happen when upward communication is repressed is something no CEO wants to contemplate, and yet many management teams create a repressive atmosphere where no avenue is provided for information access. One junior executive in a now-defunct insurance company was particularly astute and conscientious about his company's procedure. He spotted what seemed to him very peculiar goings-on in certain of the company's major agencies, but there were no established, or even informal, communication pathways open to him for reporting his observations to management. He kept his growing suspicions to himself, and by the time they were generally observable at the company's board level, the company's situation was irretrievable. So, unfortunately, was this employee's job.

Another reason for keeping communications open with lower-echelon employees—foremen or people on the line—is that often these men and women are attuned to individual operations in a way that vice presidents can't be. Sometimes these people can alert you to unrest or unhappiness that might otherwise go undetected by management until it reached stress proportions. By staying in touch with the blue-collar workers, it's often possible to check operational troubles before they get out of hand.

A management organization that encourages informal participation by lower-echelon executives, as well as by middle management personnel, is in a position to make better decisions. Such communication can be possible only where all employees, from the most junior people, have reassurance that there will be no recriminations for candor. Most people in responsible positions are eager to communicate if they are assured their heads will not be on the block.

Finally, in the all-too-frequent crisis situations, it is the dedication and extra effort that people on the line are willing to give to a responsive manager that can mean the difference between successful completion of a project and its failure. We've seen cases where angry employees have, through deliberate lack of cooperation or enthusiasm, put stumbling blocks in the way of project completion because they've resented the high-handed tactics of some junior executive. Every employee is a person sensitive to the treatment he or she receives, and responsive to it. Every employee is an important person in the company's chain of success. The manager who realizes this from the beginning can sidestep considerable alienation and frustration.

Retaining Perspective: Who's the Fairest in the Land?

A big problem for many an impatient young executive, especially one who is creative, is that his or her enthusiasm and intense energy virtually spill over, scattering ideas to the wind. If portions of these ideas form the basis for some plan put forward by a superior, later the ambitious and competitive young executive may become enraged over what seems to be the theft of an idea. One response could be to confront the offending superior. In such a confrontation, the wronged junior executive would invariably lose, either being fired or put in a position where the only option would be to resign. Alternatively, the idea person could go over the superior's head with the tale of woe, but the result would probably be the same. While the injustices of the situation are all too apparent to the irate newcomer, he or she could be failing to acknowledge that despite the so-called plagiary, the offending boss had actually provided the opportunity for creative performance. The boss's experience might even have helped to implement an idea that couldn't otherwise have worked.

Faced with the frustrations of growing in a new career, it is important for you as a young executive to weigh all the evidence concerning your own and others' contributions. Particularly, you should be candid about assessing how much of any contribution is exclusively yours. More often than not, it has been our experience that teamwork is required to perform successfully in any business function. You should always ask yourself if your astronomical ego is keeping you from seeing the part others play in the successful development of your "unique" ideas.

Further, as a new executive you should always question whether credit for a particular idea or project is more important than the opportunity to explore and develop future projects, as part of your whole career growth profile involving this company. Remember, a person who is truly creative and genuinely talented will usually be noticed and rewarded, because creativity is seldom a one-time event. Of course, if such notice should not be forthcoming over a reasonable period of years, you would be foolish not to leave and find a situation where your talent would be more readily appreciated.

We know one young man who secured a management position in a major corporation. His recent experience illustrates our point. For about five years he had worked as an assistant to a prominent executive. He had always felt superior to his boss, and had frequently become angry and impatient that their positions were not reversed. The boss decided to start his own company, and invited his young subordinate to join him in the new enterprise. Instead, our young friend elected to stay on with the corporation, seeing the coveted opportunity to fill the position his boss had vacated. Once having achieved his "rightful" place, he lasted only a matter of months before, by mutual agreement, he moved on to another company. What he realized by then was that he had failed to give his former boss credit for his real managerial talent. Left on his own, the young executive discovered many heretofore unsuspected holes in his own abilities.

When it comes to assessing abilities, it is important that you as an aspiring executive be scrupulously honest and objective about yourself *and* about the people with whom you work. Sometimes airing opinions, problems, and frustrations to a spouse or another A-Friend may permit greater detachment, revealing that you are on an unacknowledged ego trip that may, in fact, lack justification in the real world.

Leadership vs. Interpersonal Relationships

No matter how aware, and how careful, you as a leader may be in using the time resource, clearly your interpersonal relationships will be sacrificed to some extent. As the job pressures grow, and your contributions to the corporation become more significant, both time commitments and your personal priorities are bound to be affected. This is one reason why open communication will be so important within your leadership family. If at any time the pressures become unbearable for any member of your family, or if your long-range goals are perceived as insufficient compensation for your immediate sacrifices, then your family's leadership orientation should be seriously reconsidered, and perhaps abandoned in favor of a more realistic set of expectations and demands. Constant dialogue among all members of your family is essential to ensure continuing active commitment to leadership goals. Such dialogue can keep family communication dynamic, minimizing deterioration or stagnancy, and avoiding polarization of ideologies and goals.

One reason for difficulty in maintaining family relationships will be the pressure of adding responsibility for the overall corporation. As an executive moving up the corporate ladder, you will be assuming increasing responsibility for other lives, and their ultimate dependency on you.

As one industrial leader explains it, as a business executive he knows that each job in his company sustains five people in the community. Maintaining his company at full employment strength of 33,000 people requires $7 million worth of business every day. Naturally, he feels constant, enormous pressure. Even though on an intellectual level he knows he isn't indispensable at work, he *feels* that he is. He is so burdened with the problems of his company, and of the employees who demand his personal interest and attention, that there is a tendency to consider secondary the problems and demands of his own family. By the time he gets home, he is saturated with people, and just wants to be left alone. So he must be on guard constantly against a "god complex," on the one hand, and on the other a tendency to withdraw from family and friends, and to consider their attention as invasions of his privacy.

On top of these pressures there is for most executives the ever-present threat of failure, and a constant awareness of inevitable obsolescence. Every executive knows that nobody is easier to fire than a president. And a fired president's marketability is at a low ebb: most companies do not want an executive who is a recent failure. Faced with all this, the executive can develop an insatiable need for continuing evidence of success and personal importance which, in a vicious circle, excuses or justifies reduced emphasis on family priorities.

A positive corollary of this pressure is the enormous satisfaction that comes to an executive who devotes time and energy to encouraging and contributing to the growth and success of subordinates who go on to fulfill their own leadership roles.

A Leadership Trap: The Great "I Am"

Executive, company, and family pressures, coupled with growing civic and social responsibilities, can distort perspectives—often with disastrous results. The leader may become so convinced of his or her importance that ego gratification replaces sound judgment. An example that we've watched recently comes from a major corporation that is going through a tremendous upheaval because two of its principles, and several board members, are so hell-bent on their own ego trips. None of the executives involved in the struggle wants to give an inch for fear of sacrificing personal sovereignty and corporate power. As a consequence, the company is floundering. This could be a loss to its many employees and stockholders. Ego involvement is one of the most insidious and destructive problems facing leaders. The hardest decision making of all may well be that relating to empire building. Enormous strength and security are required to decide against personal aggrandizement for the good of the total organization. Many bad decisions are made because a leader lacks these qualities which are essential to healthy, rational leadership.

Another pitfall of leadership ego is the reluctance to acknowledge a bad decision. A leader who, in the face of all evidence, insists he or she was right and the world wrong, is courting disaster for the organization. The influences of IT and time compression will soon force executives to change such behavior, because judgmental errors will be amplified in the sense of full disclosure. The executive capable of saying "I was wrong. Let's change our program right now, before it affects the entire company," will be the survivor. Such an executive will have the capacity to use the very IT tools that exposed the error to rectify it immediately, while relatively little damage has occurred.

Still another danger stemming from the ego involvement of a leader can result from a misconception of his or her power. A successful executive or other leader must constantly be on guard against this booby trap, which can lead to a belief that all the deference and admiration afforded his or her professional accomplishments is deserved in any area. Obvious examples are successful film stars, astronauts, and athletes, whose great public stature confuses them into believing they are competent to act as political pundits, art experts, literary critics, and general arbiters of taste and morals. Business executives and politicians are just as human, and just as prone to believe their own notices, extending themselves beyond their areas of competence with sometimes negative results.

One example we know involved an executive friend who had built up a large and very successful manufacturing conglomerate. Gradually he became convinced that his very considerable managerial talents would enable him to run *any* business with equal success. He invested in a large retail business and proceeded to demonstrate total inability to function in that field. His misconception of himself resulted in a considerable financial loss, from which he was fortunate to recover with sufficient capital to return to the manufacturing area where he was indisputably a star performer.

The Peter Principle, of which he certainly was a victim, is harder on leaders than on less ambitious members of society. Consequently, leaders must be constantly on guard against being led by their egos beyond their areas of competence.

In a balanced family there is a built-in protection against the "pompous ass" syndrome that characterizes a runaway ego. Because each member of such a family is encouraged to become a whole ME, there is less danger of ego hangups, and greater freedom to recognize and acknowledge errors and wrong decisions without loss of esteem. In a family where equal weight is given to all members' contributions, communication becomes easier and the leader is less likely to fall into an autocratic role either at home or at work.

Assessing the Rewards of Leadership: Is It All Worthwhile?

As the dynamic process of goal and value assessment occurs within the balanced executive family, each member should consciously consider the long-term rewards that may follow, compared with the many immediate sacrifices required. The leader and all the other family members should be involved in determining whether the actual and potential gratifications of the leadership role justify the many demands. Rewards of leadership should be examined and discussed by the spouses and the entire family.

Historically, the most obvious and traditional rewards of high executive (or other leadership) status have been wealth and power. Affluence, if not itself a goal, has at least been a fairly common adjunct to leadership status. Power to influence decisions and to direct, to a degree, the lives and future courses of people and institutions has been an equally common reward of leadership.

Even with new tax laws and more stringent legal restrictions on executive compensation mechanisms and other perquisites of business success, we may still see instant millionaires among the ranks of successful business executives. Financial rewards may be less immediate and tangible, taking the direction of profit sharing and retirement plans, medical and life insurance protection, education funds for executives' children, and other fringe benefits geared to long-term economic security for the executive and his family.

Increasingly, we believe, the avenue for achieving immediate personal affluence will be tied less directly to the company's performance, and will become more the direct responsibility of the executive family—as entrepreneurs and private investors acting in their own behalf. Whether immediate or deferred, from direct compensation or investment, there are still financial rewards for a successful career as a business leader. One thirty-year-old entrepreneur recently told us, "The government takes an awful lot —but look how much is left!" In our opinion there will be more opportunities for business success in the 1980's than have been available during the past several decades.

Many young leaders seem to be less interested in "money for its own sake" than in the other rewards of success. Some young professional managers derive gratification from the fact of participation—from influencing institutions to act ethically and with social conscience, from being where the action is, and from interacting with other people and other institutions to effect positive change. Many executives of the future will view financial success less as a way to achieve total material comfort than as a vehicle to do many other things that they believe to be more important. Their utilization of affluence, rather than being related to instant gratification, will be part of their adaptation of a new system of goals for their families.

Some business leaders will want to become capital venturers and investors in new companies. They will have the foresight to recognize that dynamic business development is tomorrow's frontier, just as moving west represented the frontier for the nineteenth century. The risks are different, but as was true in the nineteenth century, there are always those willing to risk exploring new frontiers, whatever form they take. In the nineteenth century, the risk takers were rewarded by being among the early settlers to whom America's natural resources offered great wealth. In the last quarter of this century, the frontier people will be those in dynamic business development who will risk capital, rather than lives. Their rewards will come from returns on their investments, rather than from natural resources. Among tomorrow's risk-takers will be new institutions, created and directed by today's seasoned entrepreneurs and executives, which will be geared toward encouraging the growth of new businesses, and the development of new opportunities for Americans in all walks of life.

Whatever the direction of his or her individual career, every executive must still face a critical period of evaluation and redirection. This decision making period has to do with getting out: moving to a new position within the same company, to a new company or industry, moving into a totally different professional area, or perhaps retiring from corporate life. This is an especially crucial period in the lives of both marriage partners and should be recognized as such, and planned, for, well in advance of the actual crisis.

EXECUTIVE FUTURE CHALLENGES

We hope you've started thinking about the process of becoming professionalized as a leader. Think about these situations in terms of the leadership tools available to you.

1. You've just joined an organization as a manager. You're replacing the founder and developer of the company, and you've been brought in from outside. Everyone else in the management structure was selected and trained by the person whose job you're assuming. You have no established loyalties, and it's clear to you that the company has been badly mismanaged. Throughout the company you are met with open suspicion and hostility. How do you handle yourself and the problem?

2. You're a young woman executive who has recently been hired by a large and well-known company. You were hired along with a group of young men, and have gone through the company's training program. Now you have been placed in a responsible management position that makes you the boss not only over several of these colleagues, but over a number of older men who have seniority in the company. While they are overtly cooperative, they are covertly undermining you in an attempt to demonstrate that you're not capable of handling the job. How do you approach the problem?

13

The Leadership Career in Transition

The moment of truth about moving on—or out—can occur at almost any stage of an executive career. For many executives, this particular developmental change is a fact of aging and getting tired of the demands of a leadership role. For others it comes when the level of success in a particular company or industry has put the executive beyond the point of feeling challenged or excited by his or her present career. For some it happens with recognition that there is no room for them at the top of a particular organizational structure. Others may face the decision concerning whether—and where—to move when they have reached a level or a position in which they are no longer competent to perform, or when they simply feel stale in a particular role of industry. Some executives may be forced to make a decision about moving because they face a corporate policy decision that is in conflict with their personal ethic. A lucky few may decide to move on because they are in great demand in another company or in another leadership area, such as academia or government. And finally, current changes in our nation's industrial infrastructure—such as energy and steel—may force leaders to seek new opportunities and different frontiers.

Whatever the circumstances surrounding the particular crisis, it is often difficult for the executive to analyze his or her own situation and to decide when the time has come to make a *move,* and what the nature of the *move* should be. This is another of the many occasions in the life of an executive couple when an US relationship can greatly enhance the executive's decision making. A sensitive and supportive spouse, accustomed to communicating about the fears, frustrations, and successes of the leader's career, is in a position to empathize in trying times and can often bring a clearer perspective to a difficult situation than can the executive who is experiencing it.

To Move or Not to Move: Weighing the Options

The decision to move becomes more difficult as the executive grows older, and so does the move itself. The executive whiz kid at thirty-five has more options and fewer qualms than does a fifty-year-old vice president with a proven track record. The young executive, when frustrated by the conservative tradition of the corporation, concerned about corporate ethics, or simply stifled at the prospect of waiting years for the next promotion, stands to lose relatively little by looking around for greener pastures. Even if the greener pastures represent a high-risk situation, the young executive may feel the potential gain far outweighs long-term security.

A senior executive with fewer productive years ahead, and with past accomplishments having earned both affluence and a substantial vested interest in the present position, naturally feels somewhat more hesitant about seeking any dramatic change, however unsatisfactory the status quo. Such an executive may be far more tolerant of frustration and more inclined to rationalize conflict and dead-end situations than a young and still rising executive would be. Often both the headstrong young "turk" and the cautious veteran executive need the understanding and encouragement of an honest, sensitive, and well-informed observer—a spouse, an A-Friend of the same sex, or, ideally, both —in analyzing their situations.

Whatever the age of the executive debating a move, an important consideration should be his or her present role in the corporate structure. If a move seems to be in the cards, it's smart to make it when still on the upward slope. Once having peaked in a particular company, or worse, started downhill, the executive has both fewer options and less self-confidence.

It is important for every executive to develop analytical abilities that allow fair assessment of contributions to a given corporation, and the reception given to his or her ideas and leadership. This analysis should involve not only personal abilities and contributions, but also a candid evaluation of other executives in the corporation, at the same level, and above. If upper management is young, vigorous, and successful, advancement will obviously come more slowly than if he or she is being groomed by senior executives who are approaching retirement age. If two or three other junior executives seem to have an inside track with top management, a young executive may be kept on ice for an indefinite period. After a self-ranking in terms of the existing and potential power structure, the executive must decide if his or her career will benefit more from being patient and playing a waiting game, or from forcing the situation by moving. This involves an honest and unemotional examination of goals, including the big question: Does he or she *really* want to be a top banana, or will a less risky and less rewarding role suffice?

Sometimes this is the most difficult decision an executive ever makes, and it is important that both marriage partners be involved in a frank goal assessment. A great deal of unnecessary conflict and pain can be spared when both members of an executive couple are in agreement about limiting their career aspirations. For example, a wife who continues to push her husband because she doesn't understand the change in his professional orientation can unwittingly undermine him. On the other hand, a wife who shares the decision and extends love and support to her executive husband as a respected human being can soften the pain of acknowledging self-limitations.

When a move is being considered and discussed, the executive's self-analysis should include a candid assessment of personal strengths and weaknesses, and their relative importance in the present corporation, in the industry in which he or she now works, in other corporations and industries, and in totally different endeavors. As an example, a young woman executive with strong management skills, but a limited technological background, may find herself dying on the vine in a sophisticated electronics company, and yet her managerial talents would be of inestimable value in some other field. If she can honestly perceive her own limitations, and recognize that they are limitations only in her present context, she can better apply her very positive abilities to a more satisfying and potentially rewarding career.

The difference between outstanding success and dismal failure may lie in the executive's capacity to analyze personal abilities and use them in an area where they are valued. What is crucial here is the executive's ability to assess the situation and to act *before* his or her hand is forced, to seize an opportunity to apply professional skills in the area where they'll be most useful, rather than trying to find a niche after being rejected.

Moving doesn't always mean leaving an industry or even a particular company. Increasingly, large corporations that have spent both years and dollars developing young professional managers are eager to see these executives used most effectively within the corporation. These companies recognize the loss involved in letting a trained executive go into the outside world with skills that might be gainfully applied to a specialized area within the corporation. Many conglomerates, in particular, choose to stimulate young executives and keep them on the team by turning over to them the development of subsidiary companies or new and innovative programs. This way younger managers can be moved up quickly, without waiting for the older executives to retire from the scene. Similarly, older executives who may be falling behind in technological or other rapidly changing areas may be reassigned to roles where their skills are not obsolete but are badly needed. Again, either a young or an experienced executive who understands his or her personal strengths and weaknesses can help to bring about such moves, thereby avoiding getting stuck in a position where he or she will either become bored or will demonstrate incompetence.

Often, an executive does *not* have such self-awareness, and is seen in a poor light, thus losing the opportunity to take the initiative in finding a new position. Depending upon the position within the organization, the extent to which he or she has fallen into disfavor, and the basic corporate personality, the situation may be handled in a variety of ways. The executive may be fired outright or may be advised to seek employment elsewhere while he or she still has the benefits of employment (secretarial help, etc.); he or she may be subtly ignored and excluded from policy meetings, informal sessions, and social gatherings; or may be reassigned to some lesser position that leaves no recourse but to resign. Alternatively, the executive may be transferred to another desirable position that better utilizes his or her proven skills. If he or she stands high enough in the corporate hierarchy, the executive may be promoted up and out to a level where he or she can't affect the actual operations of the company, but where the prestige and all the perquisites of a top management position are retained. The higher the level of the executive, of course, the more delicate the problem becomes for those who are dissatisfied with his or her performance. In the case of a company president who is no longer functioning in a competent manner, it becomes the onerous task of the board of directors to attempt to resolve the situation. The problems of face-saving within the company, and in contacts with other corporations and executives, becomes a very touchy one. Whatever the circumstances of the particular executive who reaches a personal level of incompetence, as defined in *The Peter Principle*,* it is obviously preferable to make the discovery and to *take* appropriate action, before such action is forced!

The Executive As Adventurer—"Branching Out"

Changing jobs, companies, or industries can advance an executive career, or keep it from regressing. Another kind of executive move involves branching out into new career areas, either simultaneously with, or in succession to, the original leadership career. In a way, such branching out is a natural outgrowth of a leadership personality: a dynamic, ambitious individual who has achieved success in one career needs new challenges and stimulation, and

* Laurence J. Peter and Raymond Hull, *The Peter Principle: Why Things Always Go Wrong,* 1969. Morrow.

often finds them in exploring some new professional avenue. An executive who has succeeded and achieved recognition in one leadership area has the confidence (and the need for ego gratifications) to try his or her hand at something new and different. The combination of natural ambition and adventurousness that helped him or her to succeed in the first career, coupled with a strengthened sense of his or her own abilities, can spur a leader on to explore new and sometimes quite divergent areas of endeavor. Politics, academia, the media, the popular arts, and even religion are among the areas in which proven leaders frequently seek new careers.

Usually the innate drive to try something new is fed by some dissatisfaction with the status quo: boredom with a secure position, or chagrin at having his or her creativity and vision focused on someone else's problems may lead an executive into entrepreneurial pursuits. Disenchantment with the social role of his or her institution, or its lack of relevance, may stimulate another leader to enter a field in which he or she can serve society. Someone who is frustrated by what he or she sees as his or her organization's resistance to good technological change may seek a consulting situation where he or she can present innovative ideas to many organizations and influence their decisions. Other highly creative and dynamic individuals who become frustrated by red tape and going through channels may look for a professional situation where they can force direct action.

For some leaders who have achieved great wealth along with their success, branching out into new areas represents one way to distribute that wealth so that it can continue to work for the good of society. We have all benefited from some of the branching out activities undertaken by certain leaders who have amassed great fortunes—such as the Rockefellers, the Fords, the Mellons, and the Whitneys. Others who have achieved great wealth may not be household names, and their contributions to society, education, and the arts may be less well known, but they have also felt the obligation imposed by their privilege. Many programs for encouraging small businesses, for developing professionals among minority members willing to work in their home communities, for educating the disadvantaged, for civic enrichment, and for curtailing environmental destruction are a direct result of branching out activities undertaken by such leaders.

Whatever the motivations of a particular executive or other leader branching out into a new career area, the move itself frequently involves greater risks, and also potentially greater rewards (whether economic, social, or emotional), than would staying exclusively in the original professional role.

In an earlier chapter we discussed one danger inherent in the leadership role, and that is the tendency of some leaders to believe in their own infallibility in all things—to develop a "god complex." The time when any leader starts to think about branching out into new fields of endeavor is one time when this danger is very acute. A spouse who is sensitive to this possibility can often spot danger signs in the leader, and can help to distinguish between a genuine opportunity to apply real talents in a new and promising professional venture and a potentially hazardous situation that is appealing only because of the chance to prove a secret suspicion that he or she can do *anything* well! Depending upon who does it, how, and why, branching out into multiple careers can prove rewarding, therapeutic, or disastrous for the individual leader and his or her family. It should be approached with the same self-awareness and frank communication that we have urged with respect to moving into a new job, company, or industry.

Knowing When to Quit—Gracefully

Every leader must eventually face the decision of when to give it all up: when, consciously, to decide that he or she can best serve self, family, and the interests of the business or other institution by stepping out of the picture. One way is to set an arbitrary limit: age or some personal measure of staying on top of things. The difficulty with this approach is sticking to it when the times comes. As the leader hits the magic age, or fails to measure up to a personal standard of performance, he or she is also feeling the ego threats of his or her diminishing worth, fading youth, and limited future, and this may be the very time the need to cling to leadership status is most acutely felt. At the present time in our own society we can see outstanding examples of business giants who have changed their own rules concerning mandatory retirement in order to stay at the helm of their respective industries. Their own majority control of the stock ensures their tenure, and they have in effect created monarchies for themselves, whatever the consequences to the business, and the stifling or loss of younger management talent.

In general, leaders facing the prospect of relinquishing their active status fell into two categories: those who at least say they want to get out at the peak of their powers and accomplishments, leaving behind an untarnished and possibly unbeatable record of performance, and those who admit to wanting to die in the traces, with the vague hope that death will take them in their prime, rather than when their abilities are visibly declining.For both categories; the loss of leadership status represents an undeniable threat, and there seem to be few shining examples of leaders who have made the transition successfully and happily.

This problem is especially acute for contemporary and for budding leaders, because IT and time compression are combining to force earlier achievement of leadership status, accompanied by earlier obsolescence of any given leader, and earlier and earlier forced retirement. The extremity of the situation is typified in current politics: a young and dynamic leader such as Jerry Brown, in his early forties the governor of California and would-be presidential candidate, will probably reach the peak of his career in mid-forties, and will have exhausted his tenure as "top banana" by his mid-fifties. Only a score of years ago that age would have been considered about the right time for a politican to begin aspiring to the presidency, and yet we may see future presidents who are "respected senior statesmen" (a euphemism for has-beens) at fifty. While their plight is less visible, entrepreneurs who build their own companies on the strength of their personal abilities often achieve dramatic success and full-scale leadership at quite an early age. Yet, as the company matures, the visionary, risk-taking brilliance of the entrepreneur may not be suited to the careful management of a going enterprise, and the still young entrepreneur may have to step aside to make room for a new type of manager with skills more directly relevant to the company's emerging needs.

Obviously, it will become increasingly important to our society not to waste the special talents of trained leaders of any age who face retirement from their particular careers. Programs must be developed to refocus their creative energies. Some companies have attempted to enact such programs, by encouraging retiring executives to continue to use offices on the company premises to direct part-time community-oriented activities, or to act as advisors to the company. We've seen some fairly satisfactory retirements achieved by leaders who have been able to transfer their unique capabilities, special interests, and abundant energies to some other area of endeavor—branching out after retirement.

Recognizing the potential frustration and conflict implicit in staying close to companies that they once managed, some retiring executives choose to apply their abilities to helping new companies get established, acting either as board members or as major investors. Others lend their management skills to small businesses in need of expert advice, or become active in youth organizations, in setting up special programs within developing nations, in community and social services, or in assisting hospitals and religious organizations faced with growing business and personnel problems. Many of these executives who lend their talents as emeritus advisors can afford to do so because they have retired from corporate life with freedom from financial worry. This retirement with dignity allows them to extend their usefulness to society, and their own satisfaction in performing valued tasks. And a variety of business, social, and governmental institutions can profit by having access to managerial talents they could not possibly afford to hire from younger leaders, still involved in their most financially productive years.

While more traditional forms of retirement are still available —extensive travel, pursuit of artistic talent, involvement in leisure activities, and even full-time residence in a leisure community designed for affluent retired persons with similar social and athletic interests—these offer little promise of fulfillment for younger and still energetic retirees. We must come to recognize the development of meaningful alternatives for retiring leaders as a social imperative for the information society where incredible demands are made upon leaders who are rewarded with prominence and wealth, and then abandoned when they have reached their peak. This situation is destructive not only for the leaders and their families, but also for the society that discards the still valuable skills that leaders have so painstakingly developed.

Throughout this book, we've talked about leaders and leadership. Our focus has always been on the business executive and his or her family. Now let's look closely at the ways in which business leaders can influence our society.

EXECUTIVE FUTURE CHALLENGES

While these special challenges may seem very far away, the pressures of changing—and ending—a leadership career will almost certainly be part of your future. How will you, as a leadership family, handle it? Because, as you grow older, your approaches to various management problems may change, it is important to keep discussing attitudes, and to be aware of these subtle changes and their implications.

1. As a business executive you've spent the last ten years climbing the executive ladder. At thirty-five, you feel you can rise no further. You recognize that you've become obsolete through a combination of time compression and technological advances. Now you must decide whether to stay where you are in essentially a static position, whether to move to another company where your obsolescence will not be immediately apparent, or whether to retrain yourself in another career where perhaps you can avoid becoming out of date so quickly. What do you do?

2. You have passed the age of sixty, and have also passed the peak of your career. You know that retirement is imminent, yet you cannot realistically face this problem. Which of the many management tools we've discussed will help you to solve this problem? How would you use them.?

14

The Emerging Leader

Now is the time to ask yourselves one key question. Do you, as a family, believe in the private enterprise system? Do you believe that capitalism can be a constructive force in a democracy? Because if you don't you'd better opt out of your executive future! If you *do* believe in the future of private enterprise, and the improvement of our capitalistic system, it's time for your personal involvement and dedication!

If you are truly committed to the life of leadership described in this book, the time to start taking social responsibility is *now*. As you take your first step up the professional ladder as a business leader, you are also embarking on your career as a leader in society. What this means to you is immediate, conscious involvement in the leadership role. For openers, there is no room in your life for a double standard of conduct—personal and professional integrity must mesh because the spotlight will be on you. The standards you easily apply to today's leadership, you'll also have to apply to yourself. As a leader, you can't deplore cheating and then turn around and cheat—personally, professionally, or socially.

Business can't wait for somebody else to take responsibility, nor can business institutions continue to react to change initiated by vocal special interest groups representing factions opposed to capitalism and democracy.

For years too many business executives have remained passive while they've gotten a bad press in the news and entertainment media. It's time now to get active. If our system is to continue along the lines established in our Constitution, "to promote the general welfare," business institutions will be required to cooperate with academic, cultural, and scientific institutions to meet societal goals.

And when we say "business can't wait," we mean *you*, as a young business leader, can't wait. As one of the new breed of business leaders you will become a role model to fill a recognized void in our total institutional leadership. Your behavior and your attitudes—as an individual and as an executive representing all of the business community—will be subject to the closest scrutiny and harshest criticism. And your behavior and attitudes had better reflect real conviction because you will be held accountable for them, both morally and legally.

It is important to note that small businesses, those with fewer than a hundred employees, have provided the bulk of employment in the United States in the past ten decades. Entrepreneurs who started new companies by developing new technology have brought about important economic and social changes in this country. At the same time, American multi-national companies have helped to redistribute capital as well as technology to developing nations. On the other hand, there have been leaders who have abused the system and also those who have failed. Knowing this, it is important for those who want to become responsible leaders of the future, to be aware of the many different ways of achieving healthy goals. To be *aware* is the first step in determining what means are necessary to produce benefits for corporate good and the general welfare.

Starting at the Bottom

If you want to argue that, as a middle-management-level executive you will have no clout to change your own organization, let alone other institutions, let us contradict you. As you select the company with which you will start your career as a business executive, one of your criteria should be an ethical posture, and ideally a social awareness, that corresponds to your own. In such an organization your own social leadership will make a positive impression, and will encourage others around you—on every level—to become aware and active as representatives of the business community in the larger society.

And then let's look at some of the social organizations on which you, as a young business executive, can have an impact. First are professional organizations allied to your career. Others are local political organizations. Youth groups, churches, community volunteer organizations are all good places to begin making your mark as a responsible business leader interested in strengthening all of our social institutions.

If all of this seems simplistic and naive—how can you change society by being a Boy Scout leader?—blame your skepticism on your graduate education in business. Too little time is devoted in graduate schools to the role of business institutions in society—the responsibility of business to society, and of society to business. Little effort is made to train budding executives to develop their leadership skills in social institutions, as well as in business, if they hope to be a positive force for a constructive capitalistic society.

One recent MBA demonstrated his leadership awareness by grasping the potential for directing his business abilities outward —and then acting on his perceptions. Following his MBA, he attended law school, where he also starred academically. He then returned to his hometown, and started off modestly enough at a local bank. Within four years he had reorganized the bank, and made a substantial amount of money for the bank and for himself. Having established himself as a young man on the way up in the community, he then directed his interest to the local Chamber of Commerce, suggesting that the institution, seldom seriously considered as a force in society, start to exercise some social responsibility. He soon organized a number of Chambers at the local level and attracted attention statewide. Addressing the State Chamber of Commerce, he was able to excite the interest of small businessmen throughout the state and incidentally, to win the governor's notice. The governor of this state recently appointed him to the State Arts Commission.

This young man saw an opportunity to broaden his business leadership skills and he seized it. And just a few years out of school he is already embarked on a socially responsible leadership career and has already done a great deal to create a positive image for business in a broad social context. He has also personally projected in a positive manner himself as a responsible leader within his community and state.

As a business leader, this young man has illustrated two of our favorite truisms. First, if you want to see a change in a social institution, or in society as a whole, get into it. Second, the way to bring about change is to think about it constantly, and then to act. _Good_ change must be planned and executed with personal dedication.

The more deeply you become involved in responsible social leadership, the more complex and challenging such leadership becomes. Institutions in transition have no guidelines to follow except your own moral and ethical persuasion. And there are no guarantees. But just as brilliant young entrepreneurs can derive excitement and satisfaction from finding new, previously undiscovered, frontiers in business and investment, so creative leaders can find stimulating and rewarding frontiers in organizing and shaping interrelationships among social institutions, including business and government.

And of course your leadership career in institutions outside your profession will progress as will your business career. Your sphere of influence will extend to institutions of broader scope and larger geographic significance. With greater involvement will come greater responsibility and greater risk. The opportunities to compromise—to choose the convenient or popular path—will be more frequent and probably more tempting. In every institution there are hard choices, leadership dilemmas. But, remember, just as in your business career, in your social leadership career you will also find yourself growing and changing through experience, and better able to deal with the challenges that face you. The top leader you will be in a few years will be a different person from who you are today: probably lonelier, perhaps harder, but certainly wiser and better prepared to recognize and to cope with the realities of business and social leadership for the general welfare.

In your multidimensional role as a social leader, as in all other facets of your future, you will not be an isolated individual, but rather a member of a leadership family. Your recognition and acceptance of broadening social responsibility must be shared with your spouse and children. The ideal is a new generation, conscious from early childhood of the interrelationships of social institutions, and the obligations of leaders to help mold these institutions into a cohesive and positive society.

In our complex, pluralistic society many leaders are required at many levels. We must forget outmoded conceptions of the man on horseback who inspires us all, setting the direction for our institutions, establishing priorities of action, and then making them work. Our top leaders may still set our directions, and establish our priorities, but it's up to us, as a cadre of leaders at all levels and in all institutions, to make the system work.

The View from the Top

Just as you, as leaders entering the business community, will have a role in molding other institutions in our society, so will leaders already at the top of the business ladder. The role of the nation's executive officers is changing rapidly. Chief executive officers are called upon not only to lead their firms as professional managers, but also to lead the business community by advocating the interests of the private sector in the development of public policy. CEOs are being held accountable for their firms' public positions as well as for their firms' resources.

Some corporate leaders are already fulfilling this new role by publicly asserting the priorities of private enterprise. We suggest that, to be most effective, the activities of these leaders be concerted and their experiences shared to benefit the business community as a whole. Already there are workshops that bring CEOs together to explore such topics of common concern as emerging corporate citizenship; the CEO and media relations; the role of private enterprise in public policy; the corporation and economic policy; the corporate agenda for tomorrow; antitrust law and effective resource management; and the corporation and society.

One essential reason why leaders at the top of the business community must extend their leadership into other social areas is that we are in an age of scarcity of resources. We face a twenty-five to thirty year period in which this resource lack will have an impact on every institution, at every level, in our society. As we have already seen, the public, rightly or wrongly, ascribes to big business the lion's share of blame for this dilemma. Big business, with existing networks of international alliances, should assume responsibility for leading us out of this period of crisis.

We should not take comfort from the fact that the public also holds government in low esteem. Rather, we should view this as a chastening indication of the general weakening of all institutions. We in business should take the first step toward strengthening the institutions of our country by forging new and solid links among business, government, labor, academia, science, and the arts.

As you can readily see, the goals we advocate here place an enormous burden on the top-level business executive. In February, 1979, Max Ways, for many years an editor of *Fortune* magazine, and for some fifty years a journalist specializing in business, addressed a business conference. In his speech, he outlined some of the techniques business leaders might employ in educating the public to the realities of American business and in stimulating multi-institutional efforts to strengthen our society.*

Mr. Ways proposes that a portion of the billions of dollars spent on TV commercials might be directed toward a more positive portrayal of the business community. He suggests that "an evening of TV commercials taken in their awful accumulation constitutes a self-mutilation of the collective corporate image. Some of the cost could be diverted to quiet explanations of business facts of life, such as, why business in an inflationary period have to raise prices, or why profits are good for labor and consumers."

Further, Mr. Ways thinks that business leaders should address themselves to some social realities not well understood by the public, such as the wide distribution of power and decision making

* Max Ways, keynote address to members of the Institute for Constructive Captalism Conference, Keystone, Colorado, February 21, 1979.

responsibility in today's corporate world. Business should actively acquaint the public with "its practical contributions toward decent, cooperative relations between people." Someone should take responsibility for portraying the "meritorious but dull aspects of business" to counter the widely covered business scandals. Mr. Ways believes that business leaders themselves must stop being victimized by the undeservedly bad reputation foisted on their profession, and should start to accept "the business system as essentially legitimate and constructive."

Quietly, but vigorously, chief executive officers who share our perception of the role of today's and tomorrow's business leaders are making their mark on society. As one example, consider Felix Rohatyn who chose to leave a prestigious career in banking to help rescue New York City in the midst of its fiscal crisis in the late 1970s. His obligation to apply his expertise for social good took precedence over the rewards of continuing in his business career.

We've looked at business executives in a new leadership role in society. We should also take a look at the society in which you, as young leaders, will be directing change—and at the directions we hope this change will take!

EXECUTIVE FUTURE CHALLENGES

We hope you are convinced that great strength is required to be a socially responsible business leader. We also hope you will want to be such a leader, serving as a role model in the community, and exercising the courage of your convictions to influence positive change and to resist the irresponsible change advocated by so many interest groups in our adversary society. As a leader, how would you handle these situations?

1. You are working for a large chemical corporation that has been widely and bitterly attacked by environmentalists. Environmental groups in your community have condemned your company despite its efforts to comply with their demands. They feel your efforts have been inadequate, and they demand the closing of the plant. You realize that closing the plant will have enormous eco-

nomic consequences in the community, as well as for the corporation, because you employ thousands of local workers. How do you, as a representative of the company, influence the community at large to understand your point of view? How do you project the company's position over the vocal outcry of the special interest groups?

2. If you believe in responsible capitalism, how can you—as a middle management business leader and role model—influence your corporation to take an active part in changing the public's view of big business? What techniques would you propose for turning a negative impression of capitalism into a positive one?

15

Promoting the General Welfare

We've explained the role of the emerging leader. Now we should look at the direction in which we believe our society can move. To explore the future intelligently, we should first examine the recent past. How has our society reached its present state of rudderlessness? How has contemporary leadership come to the current state of affairs?

How We Got Here

Let's take a look at recent history—the last couple of decades, in fact—to see how and why the leadership role has changed, and why there is, at present, an alarming void in the ranks of leaders of all our institutions. We are just beginning to surface from two decades of turmoil, and to sort out its various influences on contemporary and future society. We are acutely aware of changes in values. In place of the relatively focused and homogeneous values and aspirations of the late 1940s and the 1950s, Information Technology exposes every individual to a myriad of choices, both positive and negative. Increasingly it is left up to each individual to

151

exercise choices, rather than to follow traditional paths. At the same time, for more and more individuals, the stability and inner security that permit intelligent choice have been shaken to the roots.

Value changes may well have arisen out of the failure of most leaders to perceive that we are both an Information Society and a pluralistic society in which institutions cannot be considered, nor values formed, in a vacuum. In such a society, every leadership decision is subjected to close scrutiny, and is related to decisions in other institutions. Leaders who continued to consider the good of their own institutions in an exclusive context, or who, at best, saw the good achieved by and for their own institutions as spilling over into other social institutions, and leaders who failed to appreciate the exposure their own ideas received, were unprepared for vocal public outrage. Leaders were not—and to a great extent *still* are not—prepared to stand firm in the face of interest groups when they believe their demands to be wrong.

Few leaders so far have been sufficiently visionary to recognize and act on the need for a balance of institutions in our society. Most have failed to take positive action as traditional leadership loci change or disappear while institutions exchange roles and importance. Increasingly, wealth has lost its domination as a criterion for leadership and power as it is continuously being redistributed through the process of taxation to the middle and lower classes. We have learned in contemporary America that socialism is not the only avenue for redistribution of wealth. And business leaders, not yet ready to assume an assertive leadership role in the larger society, for the most part have failed to demonstrate that *voluntary* redistribution of wealth, through the private sector, can be a positive force for society.

Leaders can scarcely be blamed for lacking the foresight to anticipate and prevent the changes and problems that have characterized the past decades. Within memory, or even within the recorded history of American society, leaders have been able to rely on the unquestioned acceptance of clearly defined rules. Today, every rule is questioned. The leader who relies upon unqualified support for an "obvious" position is bewildered—and doomed. Not only are the rules questioned, but the right to leadership is also in dispute. "Rank hath its privileges" is now a disputed adage—and the privileges that rank hath are greatly diminished, even as the demands, responsibilities, and the *risks* of rank grow.

Where Do We Go From Here?

In the future, there will be still greater burdens placed upon leaders and their families. Leaders must understand and use Information Technology—it will be a key to performing their roles. To use and control IT will be to control other resources. If information gathering and handling displaces more interesting or amusing activities and leisure pursuits, that is just *one* sacrifice that the leadership role will extract.

New leadership will require the capacity to comprehend and help to manage simultaneous sweeping changes in a multitude of institutions. Leaders will have to be selective—advocating and promoting beneficial change while resisting negative change. Informational sophistication will be required to discern when pressures for change represent the will of a vocal minority, rather than the good of the majority.

Clearly, what we are calling for is a new dimension in leadership. The qualities of leadership we see as essential to the society of the future cannot be found in isolated individuals. They must be found through deliberately assembling groups of leaders from the full spectrum of social institutions and providing them a climate in which it is possible to work together toward common, interrelated goals. Leaders must function deliberately to achieve balance in the progress and development of those institutions.

What such interdisciplinary leadership requires is not so much the capacity to *predict* technological breakthroughs or social directions, but to choose: Which social direction benefits the majority of institutions and individual citizens? What sacrifices must be made by the majority to benefit the deprived minorities? Which demands of special interest groups are legitimate, and which are irresponsible harassment? When are certain social values to be traded off for others? These are the sorts of choices that leaders in the immediate future must face in behalf of the total society. To do this they need an abundance of noise-free data—*and* the insights gained from inter-institutional communication and participation.

What Now?

In this chapter, we have examined some of the ways in which past leadership has failed society, and some of the reasons for this failure. In preceding chapters we have proposed some of the techniques we see as essential to future leaders in avoiding these pitfalls. And we have tried to suggest as strongly as possible that you, as business executives, will have no choice but to participate in a leadership role in your career and in other social institutions.

The pressures of an Information Society, with essentially universal (and virtually instantaneous) dissemination of negatives about business—whether these negatives stem from business' own transgressions or from the unwarranted attacks of special interest groups—demand that business respond not defensively, but positively, with pride and with fervor. Business leaders must recognize that we have become an adversary society. Special interest groups can advocate anything—or attack anything—with no responsibility for their actions. Splinter groups have immunity; business does not. Business leaders must understand this distinction and must enthusiastically and deliberately embrace the opportunity to represent their own responsible position in society.

To be a leader in this new society will require enormous strength and courage. As the leadership role becomes lonelier and riskier, leaders will need as a minimum the understanding and strength of those most intimately connected to them. They will need the bolstering of an US relationship, and A-Friends. They will need the reassurance of the Umbrella Theory. They will need the active support and participation of a balanced family in their many interrelated activities.

Leaders in the future will have to forget about the rules; there is no more "right way." As attitudes, values, and laws change, leaders must be ahead of those changes. We believe that business leaders will have to lead change, not follow along behind some splinter group's carrot—or worse, ahead of its stick. They will need the inner strength and flexibility to direct change for the benefit of a balanced, interdependent society.

Leaders must be conscious role models for the rest of society. Because they will be visible, they must be prepared to live according to the ethical and moral principles they profess, or they will be instantly attacked as hypocrites.

We must recognize that in the future the business leaders will often be cast in the role of conscious victim. In a period when we are just emerging from a decade of confusion and despair, with no rules to follow and future directions not clearly marked, business leaders will sometimes be forced to make decisions and take actions without being able to predict the outcome of those actions. By acknowledging fallibility and acting to correct their mistakes, they may be able to survive the process of trial and error. But every leader in the future must face up to the responsibilities of the role in full knowledge that his or her tenure, at best, will be brief, and that the ultimate reward may not be glory, but martyrdom.

We have done what we can to prepare you, as future leaders, to meet the challenges of your business career, and of the inextricably linked role as a leader in other social institutions. We can only hope that you will weigh your own personal values and aspirations in terms of these larger commitments that come with business leadership. If you, as leaders and as family members, are not prepared for the responsibilities—and the agonies—that are part and parcel of the leadership experience, we hope that you will have the courage to alter your future course.

For those of you who decide that the rewards of leadership more than make up for the sacrifices—welcome to the world of executive families!